Layman's Bible Book Commentary
Genesis

LAYMAN'S BIBLE BOOK COMMENTARY

GENESIS
VOLUME 1

Sherrill G. Stevens

BROADMAN PRESS
Nashville, Tennessee

Dedicated to Marguerite

4211–71
ISBN: 0–8054–1171–2

Dewey Decimal Classification: 222.11
Subject heading: BIBLE O. T. GENESIS

Library of Congress Catalog Card Number: 78–050377
Printed in the United States of America

Foreword

The *Layman's Bible Book Commentary* in twenty-four volumes was planned as a practical exposition of the whole Bible for lay readers and students. It is based on the conviction that the Bible speaks to every generation of believers but needs occasional reinterpretation in the light of changing language and modern experience. Following the guidance of God's Spirit, the believer finds in it the authoritative word for faith and life.

To meet the needs of lay readers, the *Commentary* is written in a popular style, and each Bible book is clearly outlined to reveal its major emphases. Although the writers are competent scholars and reverent interpreters, they have avoided critical problems and the use of original languages except where they were essential for explaining the text. They recognize the variety of literary forms in the Bible, but they have not followed documentary trails or become preoccupied with literary concerns. Their primary purpose was to show what each Bible book meant for its time and what it says to our own generation.

The Revised Standard Version of the Bible is the basic text of the *Commentary*, but writers were free to use other translations to clarify an occasional passage or sharpen its effect. To provide as much interpretation as possible in such concise books, the Bible text was not printed along with the comment.

Of the twenty-four volumes of the *Commentary*, fourteen deal with Old Testament books and ten with those in the New Testament. The volumes range in pages from 140 to 168. Four major books in the Old Testament and five in the New are treated in one volume each. Others appear in various combinations. Although the allotted space varies, each Bible book is treated as a whole to reveal its basic message with some passages getting special attention. Whatever plan of Bible study the reader may follow, this *Commentary* will be a valuable companion.

Despite the best-seller reputation of the Bible, the average survey of Bible knowledge reveals a good deal of ignorance about it and its primary meaning. Many adult church members seem to think that its study is intended for children and preachers. But some of the newer translations have been making the Bible more readable for all ages. Bible study has branched out from Sunday into other days of the week, and into neighborhoods rather than just in churches. This *Commentary* wants to meet the growing need for insight into all that the Bible has to say about God and his world and about Christ and his fellowship.

BROADMAN PRESS

Contents

This Book Named *Genesis*

A child asks, "Mommy, where did I come from?" A curious lad wonders aloud, "Why don't snakes have feet?" or "Why do dogs chase squirrels?" Behind such questions lie concerns as profound as the meaning of life itself. Questions like these stirred the minds of ancient people. The Bible opens with some inspired answers.

The book of Genesis is a book of beginnings. That is what the word *Genesis* means. This name was given to the first book of the Bible because the first Hebrew word in the book means "in beginning." The name is very appropriate, for this book contains a record of the origins of many things in human history. Great themes such as creation, the formation of human families, and the development of human civilization are present in this book. These themes are treated with the marvelous insight of divine inspiration and the masterful beauty of artistic genius. This first part of the Bible has rare blessings for every person who will study it in seeking to understand the gracious ways of God's dealing with mankind.

Background

What do we know about the background of Genesis? Not nearly as much as we would like to know. Extensive studies have been made of the authorship and time of writing. Careful and comparative studies of the language and text of Genesis indicate that in its present form it was written probably sometime after the period of David and Solomon. The message of the book is obviously much older than that. In ancient times writing was not a common, everyday skill. The insights and heritage of the people were preserved as they were passed on by spoken word and memory from one generation to another. We can assume that much of the book had been a part of this oral tradition for a long, long time before it was put into writing.

The first five books of the Bible are known to us by their familiar names. They are also referred to as the "five books of Moses." According to an ancient tradition, Moses was the source of this significant part of the Bible. Such a tradition does not require that he was the originator of all the information in these books. He was the central figure of Hebrew history in the Exodus era and the great formulator of Hebrew law. Without doubt he was also an important gatherer of the great insights and traditions of human history up to his own time. His education in the Egyptian court prepared him to do some of the writing. This wonderful heritage continued to be preserved in oral tradition for several more generations before it was compiled and written.

God has done an amazing thing by revelation and inspiration, for he stands behind the creation of the marvelous book of Genesis. He guided those who first saw the light and truth. He guided those who told the story from generation to generation. He guided those who wrote the record and preserved it. He still guides those who study the Bible so that its message may break through as living truth.

Genesis does not stand alone, separate and apart from the rest of the Bible. It is a part of the whole and is especially part of the unit called the Pentateuch ("Five Books"). Genesis includes the pre-Hebrew and patriarchal periods. The next four books record the Exodus, Sinai, and wilderness periods of Hebrew history. The book of Joshua carries the historical record further with an account of the migration into the land of Palestine and the people's settlement there to become the Hebrew nation. Without some knowledge of the origins described in Genesis, it would be almost impossible to understand what followed. Genesis itself is understood more fully when it is seen as a part of the larger picture of God's redemptive work through the Hebrews as a chosen, covenant people. The whole picture of truth is even further enlarged by the inspired insights of the prophets and the New Testament.

Understanding Genesis

Whoever reads Genesis should remember that this entire book is not in one literary style. The book includes historical narrative. It also contains poetry (chap. 49), cultural traditions (27:1-4), genealogies (5:1-32; 10:1-32; 11:10-32), and symbolism (37:5-11; 41:1-8). A study of this book should include diligent and prayerful effort to distinguish between these varied forms of writing and to understand the truth

behind what is written. Genesis includes history, but it is not all historical narrative. The writer sometimes used figurative language, but the
significance is certainly not all symbolic. The cultural traditions had
meaning in relation to the time and place in which they were observed. Because the Hebrews were a people of vivid imagination,
their language contained many pictures and poetic expressions. All
of these factors are important to our understanding the message of
the book of Genesis. Above all, it should be remembered that this
is a religious writing. Its purpose is to tell of the acts of God and of
the relationship that exists between God and mankind. Nothing should
be allowed to obscure this central focus of Genesis.

The book of Genesis falls into two major sections. The first part is
primitive history. The second part is patriarchal history. In the first
section (chaps. 1–11) there is the beautiful record of Hebrew traditions
about the origin of the world, of humanity, and of human society in
the world. The focus of attention in this section is upon individual
persons or upon mankind in general. No special covenant nation had
been formed.

In the second section (chaps. 12–50) the origin and first development
of the Hebrew nation are recorded. The Israelites traced their national
origin to a special relationship with God. They held a strong conviction
that God had established a unique relationship with them through
his call to Abraham, his covenant with Abraham's descendants, and
his later deliverance of the Israelite tribes from Egyptian bondage.

The structure of the book does not exclude the existence of earlier
written documents in the background. Structure and language within
the book indicate quite clearly that such documents did exist and
were used by the writer of Genesis. Documentary background of
this type, however, does not diminish in any way the vital divine
inspiration that underlay the traditions and brought the book of Genesis into being.

Theological Summary

Four primary streams of theological doctrine are present in Genesis.
These reflect an advanced level of religious understanding.

The writer was inspired to write of a monotheistic God, one who
was uncreated, transcendent, and the source of all existence. God is
described as having sovereignty that reached to Haran and Egypt

as well as to Canaan. He is revealed through his activity in history and through the lives of people with whom he established a personal relation.

A high view of humanity is expressed. The creation of mankind in the image of God gave to human persons the capacity to have conscious communication with God, to worship him, and to serve him. Mankind has a sovereignty within creation, but it is always subordinate to the Creator. The nature of humanity is such that disharmony with the Creator is destructive to human personhood.

The reality of evil is clearly revealed in Genesis. The essential nature of evil is human defiance of God and disobedience to his standards of righteousness. These dimensions of evil are demonstrated in the actions of Adam and Eve in the Garden of Eden and in the words of Joseph to Potiphar's wife (39:9).

God's answer to the reality of evil is redemption. He is revealed in Genesis to be a self-disclosing God who seeks reconciliation and fellowship with errant humanity. God is revealed as the initiator of redemptive action. He reached out to Adam and Eve after their sinful disobedience. He called Abraham to be the first of a covenant people to serve God in a plan of redemption for all peoples. God continued his redemptive purpose to each succeeding generation.

Harmony of fellowship with God and restoration of reconciled fellowship with God are always based on a human response of faith and trust. Genesis sets forth a doctrine of redemption that is based on the grace of a forgiving God and the faith of trusting human persons.

Part I
History Before the Hebrews

Creation
1:1 to 2:3

The Origin (1:1-2)

God was the central figure when creation took place. The opening words of Genesis declare that truth. As we begin to read the account of creation in the Bible, we are made aware that we are reading about the origin of the universe. There was a time when nothing existed but God. There was no world of time and space. Apart from God there was nothing. We are not able to shape in our minds any idea of what it was like then. It was not a world of empty space, for emptiness had no meaning before the world of time and space came into being by God's creative action.

Before the creation of the world, God existed alone in splendid majesty. The book of Genesis reflects that it was also an exclusive majesty. Neither the world nor any other divine beings existed in that timeless, ancient past. By the time Genesis was written, people had made all kinds of idol gods to worship; but the writer of Genesis believed in the true God alone. There are no references to idol gods in Genesis except in the account of Jacob's leaving Laban's house (Gen. 31:17-35) and Jacob's taking his family to Bethel to renew a covenant with God (35:1-4).

Then God began to create the world. That was the origin of everything that belongs to time, to space, and to material things. The Bible describes the making of everything out of nothing. God started by creating all the physical elements in existence. Then he formed them into an orderly universe. The Bible does not tell us when or how God did that original creative act. It does tell us that all of creation was the work of God.

The first form of the created world was shapelessness. There was not so much a condition of disorder as an absence of order. The planets were not yet set into their orbits or the stars into their galaxies. The environment of the earth did not yet include days and nights and seasons of the year. But God was not finished. He had only begun. While the world was formless in its first state, God did not intend for it to remain that way. He did not create the world to be a disordered chaos; he made it to be an orderly universe, to be inhabited by all the living creatures he would bring into being (see Isa. 45:18). So God was watching over the world he had created: "The Spirit of God was moving over the face of the waters" (Gen. 1:2). A sense of anticipation filled the air. Something else was about to happen.

The Development of Universal Order (1:3–25)

A shapeless, unfinished world was not what God had in mind when he began the creation. God took the undeveloped world that he had brought into being and formed it into a universe of marvelous order. The Bible describes that amazing event. The simplicity of the description is reflected in the way the story is written: "And God said . . . and it was so . . . and God saw that it was good" (1:3,24–25).

God's word is described as the instrument of his creative activity. The creation and development of the universe were the result of the personal will of God. He chose to make the world. His word was the way he expressed his will. Eight times in the first chapter of Genesis we find the words "And God said. . . ." Through those statements there flowed the creative power by which God brought order out of the formlessness and filled emptiness with a universe.

This record of creation reflects the marvel of inspiration. No one was there when it happened except God. It was a long, long time before any account was written. There was no source from which this insight could come except through inspiration from God.

The writer of Genesis had no knowledge of the vast spaces of the universe filled with galaxies of stars, for he had no instruments to help him look beyond what his naked eye could see. He had no knowledge of the earth as a part of a solar system, moving in orbit around the sun. For that ancient writer, the earth was the center of the universe.

The narrative of creation is organized according to God's activities over a seven-day period. The first six days were filled with creative activity as God brought order out of chaos and developed the marvelous universe that exists. The seventh day is described as the time when the originating work was finished and God rested.

Light and darkness (1:3–5).—The first step in the creative process was the division of light and darkness. The existence of light is the first fundamental need for the existence of plant and animal life. Light and darkness were believed by ancient people to be things that exist in and of themselves. Modern scientific knowledge, on the other hand, treats light as a phenomenon that flows from some brilliant source, while darkness is seen as the absence of light. The purpose of the creation account, however, was to describe light and darkness as things created by God to establish day and night and to provide the basis for life.

Heaven and earth (1:6–8).—The second step in the emerging order of the universe was the separation of the elements to form planets, atmosphere, and space. This is described as separating the celestial waters from the planetary waters to create a firmament of atmosphere between them.

Land and sea (1:9–13).—Step 3 in the development of the earth was the formation of land masses and the gathering of surface waters into oceans and seas. On the land there began to develop vegetation. The plants and trees produced seed and fruit through which reproduction occurred and the varied species continued to develop.

Heavenly bodies (1:14–19).—During the fourth day the sun, moon, and stars appeared. This step in the unfolding universal order was evidently a further development of what God had begun on the first day. The references to separating light from darkness and day from night indicate a close relationship between these two steps. In its primeval state, as God was bringing order to the universe, the earth was immersed in a heavy mist. Light was the first element created; so as the source of the earth's light the sun must have been created at that time. Only as the atmosphere began to clear and as moisture evaporated into it did the sun appear, along with the moon and the stars.

The order of life on the earth had been brought to a new level of advancement. The heavenly bodies were to be "for signs and for seasons and for days and for years." The ancient people knew, just as we do, that day and night are created by the presence or the absence of the sun. Seasons and years are controlled by the changes and movement of the sun and moon. The process of development had been brought far enough along that the earth was ready for more varied and complex forms of life to come into being. God was creating a marvelous world.

Fish and birds (1:20–23).—The first forms of animal life were those that live in water. These are the simplest forms of life, and water was the environment best suited to their existence. Birds are a form of life more developed than fish, but less complex than mammals; so God created birds next. These creatures of the water and the air were the products of God's fifth day of creation.

Land animals (1:24–25).—On the sixth day God carried out the final stages of creation to bring the world into the state we know. On that day he created the animals that live on land. These include the reptiles (creeping things) and the highest form of animal life, the mammals (cattle and beasts of the earth). All of these forms of life were endowed with the ability to reproduce and to continue their species on the earth. But God had not yet finished. The climax was not yet reached. There was yet to come the truly unique creation of all. God would make a creature like himself; he would create mankind.

Take time to reflect on what God had done to that point. Think of what mankind has learned of the impressive order and interdependence within the world. The universe is vast, and its limitless reaches hold secrets not yet discovered by any human person. The natural laws of physical force by which the universe operates are exact and dependable. By studying the marvels of universal law and order, people have been able to develop great technical resources and to travel in space. This has been done by working in harmony with what God established, not by disregarding or violating the order he created in the world. There are intricate interrelationships among the various elements of the natural order. Life on earth is greatly influenced by the force of gravity and the movement of heavenly bodies far out in space. The different forms of life on earth are dependent upon each other. All of them are related to one another within their common environment. Our study of the relationships God established in the environment at the time of creation we call ecology.

The creation narrative in the Bible presents an artistically beautiful account of universal origins that is filled with significant insights. The writer did not intend this to be a scientific analysis of the creation process. He was far more interested in writing about *who* had made the world and *why* than about *how* and *when*. This record of the creation is a hymn of praise for the Creator. It should always be read in a spirit of reverence, for that is the spirit in which it was written. The glory of the Creator is revealed in his creation. After the development of universal order, God turned to the creation of man—a creature who could perceive the glory of his Creator and respond with personal praise.

The Beginning of the Human Race (1:26–31)

An entirely new dimension of creation is reflected in the last event of the sixth day. It was as though all that had gone before was in preparation for that crowning act. What God had made was a magnificent display of his creative power and handiwork, but nothing in the creation to that point had the capacity for personal response to and fellowship with its Creator. God's stated objective was to make a creature like himself, one superior enough to have a place of authority and control over the other creatures God had made.

Kinship with animals.—It is clear that mankind has much in common with other animal species. In the description of the creation of sea and land animals ("living creatures," 1:20,24), the same Hebrew root word is used as that which describes man ("a living being," 2:7). Human beings are of the mammal species of animal life. Their bodily organs and physical systems are quite similar to other mammals' Their birth, life, and death functions are very much like those of the other higher animals. Yet humanity is far superior to any of the other animals. Mankind was a distinct, unique creation by God. People were created to have a preeminent position within, but at the head of, all creation.

A clear distinctiveness (1:26–27).—The uniqueness of mankind is reflected in the statement "So God created man in his own image" (1:27). What does this expression mean? Surely "the image of God" does not refer to the physical, bodily form of human life. While there are physical differences between animal species, humans are not so different from the others for this to be the nature of human uniqueness. In the area of physical form, humans are more kin to other animals than to God. Recall that Jesus said to the Samaritan woman at Sychar, "God is spirit" (John 4:24).

The image of God in which mankind was created refers to those qualities of humanity that are like God's. This aspect of human life certainly includes a high capacity for intelligence and reason—that is, the ability to think God's thoughts after him. People can never equal God in this capacity, but they are so far superior to other animals in reasoning ability as to have a unique kinship with God.

Humanity's unique quality.—The area of rational intelligence is not the area of humanity's closest kinship with God, however. Mankind is like God both in the quality of personhood and in the dimension of spirit, neither of which any other form of life has. A human is essentially a "spirit-person." The essential quality that makes a person what he is lies in the inner spirit. This spirit quality of human life is directly related in kinship with God, who is pure spirit. The personal quality of human life is also directly akin to God. The capacity for making choices, for personal relationship to God, and for commitment are qualities that belong to personhood. They are traits of life that belong exclusively to the nature of humans and of God.

The moral dimension.—Creation in the image of God includes morality as a quality of human life. Since people have the capacities involved in human personhood, they also have the moral responsibility to use those abilities to achieve excellence in life. The image of God is something every human being has. It cannot be escaped or obliterated.

Human persons are more than animals. They may choose to live at the level of lower animals, but they do not cease to be human. A person can never escape the responsibility to measure up to the quality of humanness in life. At the same time, humanity was created less than divine (see Ps. 8:5). So a person cannot rise above humanness to become divine. Consequently, human beings never cease to be creatures who are subject to the sovereignty of their Creator. In creation God established both the floor and the ceiling of human life. We cannot move out of the nature of humanity in either direction. People can turn the qualities of humanness toward excellence or evil. That capability belongs to the moral nature of human personhood. The later event of the fall into sin by Adam and Eve demonstrated that that condition is universal among mankind.

Male and female (1:27–28).—With the creation of human persons, the dimension of sexuality was raised to a new level. The reproductive ability had been created in plants and animals. Distinct male and female genders are present in all of the higher forms of animal life. Of all the creation, however, the quality of sexuality is referred to only of human persons. People have sexuality as a distinctive feature of their personhood, not merely as a physical characteristic

Of plants and all other animals, the creation narrative indicates that reproduction was to be a part of life. It is a physical function of instinct and nature. To human persons, however, a specific command was given to "be fruitful and multiply." That instruction was given directly, not in a general statement as in verse 22. Human sexuality is not merely a reproductive capacity. Human reproduction is not merely a function of instinct. Sexuality is a quality of personhood, and reproduction is a matter of personal, moral choice. When God created the first human persons, he created a uniquely different kind of beings. Humanity is properly called the crown of God's creation.

Commanded to control (1:28).—Not only were people instructed to reproduce and populate the earth; they were also commanded to establish control over the earth and its resources. The dominion of people over the other animals and their development and use of earth's resources were intended as a part of God's creative plan. But that dominion did not come into being automatically. It had to be established. God's word to the first people was "Subdue it," an expression that means to conquer and bring under control. That assigned task is for people to come to terms with the universe, to learn its secrets, to harness its resources, and to share with God in the ongoing development of the earth's potential.

Humanity's place in the universe is intended to be one of sovereignty, but it is a secondary sovereignty. People are to have dominion over animals and control over earth's resources, but they are always under the supreme sovereignty of God.

People are commanded to share with God in controlling the environment in which they live, but that control is by no means to be severe or destructive. The guideline is "use but do not abuse," for we are called to develop and employ, but not to become brutal ourselves or to exploit our place in the scheme of things. True humanness involves being sensitive to the use of life's resources in such ways that the quality of life is enhanced and God is glorified. People were created to be sensitive to beauty and to delight in goodness.

Provision of food (1:29–30).—The basic pattern for food supply was vegetarian. Animals were to eat green plants, and people were to eat plants and fruits. In Psalm 104 this same theme appears: "Thou dost cause the grass to grow for the cattle, and plants for man to cultivate, that he may bring forth food from the earth" (v. 14). Apparently, the primitive paradise before the fall into sin did not include any pain or bloodshed. After the fall animal skins were used for clothing (Gen. 3:21), and animals were slain for sacrifices (4:4). Only after the flood was approval given for meat to be eaten for food (see 9:3).

God's approval (1:31).—Six times already (vv. 4,10,12,18,21,25) the writer had declared that God gave the approval of "good" to what he had created. When the creation was complete and a state of universal order had been established in the world, God surveyed what he had made and affirmed the essential goodness of all creation. He declared that it was "very good."

The Significance of the Sabbath (2:1–3)

After the completion of creation on the sixth day, the emphasis of the narrative turned to God's surcease from creative work on the seventh day. The first verse of chapter 2 indicates clearly that the completion of creation had already taken place. Therefore, the statement in verse 2 that "on the seventh day God finished his work" does not mean that God did some of the creative work on the seventh day and then began to rest. The expression "finished his work," as it is used here, evidently means that God refrained from doing any more of the creation work because it was already completed.

God's rest (2:1–2).—The focus here is upon a seventh day when God rested. Recall that Isaiah wrote of God that he is "the everlasting God, the Creator of the ends of the earth. He does not faint or grow weary" (40:28). And the psalmist sang of God, "He who keeps Israel will neither slumber nor sleep" (121:4). God rested from the particular work of creation, but he has continued to be active in his other works on behalf of the world and the people in it. Jesus said, "My Father is working still, and I am working" (John 5:17).

The reason for God's resting was not because he had grown tired from the work of creation. He rested from the work of bringing the world into being to mark the successful completion of the creative event. This did not mark a cessation of God's work, but only the surcease from the work of originating the world and forming it into an ordered universe.

The hallowed day (2:3).—The seventh day was given significance by the example of God. He hallowed the day by using it to mark the completion of the world's creation. No specific command was given here that people should observe the sabbath in any particular way. It is fitting that observance of the sabbath as a hallowed religious day grew out of this example by God. He celebrated a religiously significant event in a religiously significant way. Through the centuries believers have been moved to follow his example.

It is appropriate to note that Jesus did not command a weekly celebration of his resurrection on the first day of the week. That event happened on the first day of the week, however, and thus gave special religious significance to that day. Christians have made the first day of the week one of worship and celebration.

Other meanings.—As time went on other facets of meaning were added to the sabbath. During the Exodus, when the Ten Commandments were given, the emphasis on the Fourth Commandment was that it should be kept as a memorial of God's rest on the sabbath (Ex. 20:8–11). The commandment called for human observance of the day God rested and declared that refraining from work was the way the day should be observed.

At the end of the Exodus period, Moses reviewed the Hebrews' national history and God's laws as his last act of leadership. When he reviewed the sabbath commandment, he gave it a changed emphasis. The people of Israel were commanded to keep the sabbath as a memorial to their deliverance from bondage in Egypt (Deut. 5:12–15).

Some centuries later the prophet Isaiah wrote that, by keeping the sabbath, people could show they were people of the covenant and were committed to keeping God's covenant faithfully (Isa. 56:2–8). To refrain from work showed their trust in the care of God.

These additional meanings are outgrowths from and should not replace the original meaning of the sabbath. God ceased from the work of creation because that work was completed.

The significance of the first sabbath was a celebrative acknowledgment of God's marvelous achievement in creating the world. That significance of the original sabbath, along with the example of Jesus, provides Christians with helpful insight for observing the Lord's Day. The significance of the day is not best reflected in a legalistic requirement to avoid certain activities. Nor is the day fittingly observed by engaging in secular revelry without any acknowledgment of its religious meaning. The sabbath and the Lord's Day are best observed by celebrating what God has done in creation and redemption and by doing beautiful things such as those Jesus chose to do.

Summary.—The creation narrative began with a profoundly simple statement of God's majestic action in original creation. It ends with a declaration that God completed the creation he began and then rested to celebrate the significance of what he had done. Praise for the Creator is the central theme of this inspired account of the creative origin of the universe.

Humanity
2:4 to 4:24

The Center of Life on Earth (2:4–24)

A new emphasis began in Genesis when the story of creation was completed. In 2:4 there occurs for the first of ten times in the book the statement "These are the generations of . . . ." It marks a transition from one major division to another. In this case, as the text indicates by paragraphing, the statement could be a summary of the previous story or an introduction of the material to follow.

Two accounts of creation (2:5–23).—The following paragraph opens with the phrase "In the day" (v. 4), a phrase often used in the Bible to mean *when.* The transitional idea that stands between the divisions seems to be "when the Lord made the world, this is how it was then." The statement in the text introduces what is often called a second creation account. Chapter 2 of Genesis does tell of the forming of man, the planting of trees in a garden, and the forming of various species of animals; but this is not primarily a creation narrative. The emphasis is not on the order of creation but upon the priority of man. The focus is upon man as the center of universal order. The world is oriented toward man, for in him the created world has its most direct relation with God.[1]

There are obvious differences between facts about creation as recorded in the two accounts. In chapter 2 man is described as created first instead of last; man and woman were made at different times instead of at the same time; there is no reference to times in contrast to the six days of chapter 1; and the original state of the earth was barren desert instead of watery chaos. These differences apparently did not trouble the writer, for no attempt was made to harmonize the two accounts. Evidently, there had come to him through oral tradition these marvelous accounts of world origins that are filled with insight and that have the rich quality of divine inspiration in them. Each of them has its own splendid contribution to make. Together they give a beautiful record of God's creative majesty and of his concern for humanity, which is the highest moral peak of his creation. In this second account, the focus turns to humanity as the center of life on earth.

At the beginning of this account, the earth is described as a barren landscape with no plants growing and no hand to cultivate it. Did these insights about how God formed the world develop among a desert people? For the ancient mideastern people who lived in desert regions, the absence of water meant death. A source of water was vital to life. In chapter 2 water is described as arising from within the earth to form a mist and water the earth and to feed the rivers that were crucial to the environment of the ancient Hebrews.

Man of the earth (2:7).—Into the scene God brought man, who is described as having been formed of the earth, for the human body is composed of the same physical elements that are found in the material world. This truth was applied by Paul in his letter to the Corinthians: "the first man was from the earth, a man of dust; the second man is from heaven" (1 Cor. 15:47). People have a natural belonging to the physical environment in which they live.

God added the breath of life to the earthly body he had made, and "man became a living being." The Hebrew word that describes this characteristic of human life is *nephesh,* a word also used to describe other animals (see 1:20–21,24). God gave to humanity the physical life that is shared in common with other animals. This dimension of human life is essential for human participation in the life of the world. Without it people would not be able to interact with nature or other animal life. The nature of human distinctiveness is not revealed here, but in the earlier statement that God created man "in his own image" (1:27).

Man of the spirit.—This man, who shared with other animals the breath of life, had the unique character of having spirit. That dimension of human nature is the distinctive quality that mankind alone shares with God. Isaiah described God as being the one who "gives breath to the people upon it [the earth] and spirit to those who walk in it" (Isa. 42:5). It is the spirit that makes humanity personal and sets human persons apart from all other created things.

The ancient Hebrews divided human life into three dimensions: body, soul, and spirit. The body is physical flesh. The soul is physical life. Both of these are shared in common with other animals. Spirit is possessed by mankind alone of all creatures, as part of the human nature created by God.[2] This is humanity's kinship with God. God created persons to have a place of priority in creation, to be the center of life on earth.

An Eden to live in (2:8–9).—Because the environment out of which this story of creation comes was probably one of severe desert, a matchless expression of God's care for the newly created man was to make an oasis for him to live in. So God "planted a garden in Eden." The name Eden means "delight"; so the garden that God prepared is described as a place of beauty and fruitfulness.

Eden was not a vegetable garden but was more like a park furnished with stately trees. Vegetable gardens were common among the Hebrews, but only the wealthy and prominent people had estates in the form of parks. Eden indicated the noble prominence God gave to mankind within the scheme of creation.

The Garden of Eden was made most distinctive, however, by the presence at its center of two special trees. They were "the tree of life" and "the tree of the knowledge of good and evil." There is no indication of the nature of these trees; so their presence in the garden raises an inescapable question. Were these actual trees, or is this description of them intended as a parable dealing with the relation of man to God as he lived in the garden that God had prepared for him? This is a significant question in the light of the moral issues raised later in regard to the tree of the knowledge of good and evil.

A parenthesis about geography (2:10–14).—Before the story of man in the garden continued, a brief section was set in to deal with the

location of the garden. The description is of a great river that arose
in Eden, watered the garden, and then flowed out to divide into
four rivers, which became the primary sources for water in the world.

Two of the rivers are readily identifiable, the Tigris and the Euphrates. The other two cannot be identified with any certainty. Either
the Pishon and Gihon were symbolic of the other water sources of
the world, or major changes in the terrain of the area have occurred
since this record was written.

It should be noted also that this description of one river dividing
to become the source of four rivers is a reversal of the usual pattern
of river formation. Normally, streams rise at many sources and then
flow together to form larger and larger streams and rivers until they
flow into the sea. This description of the river in Eden becoming
the source for the major rivers of the then known world is quite
similar to descriptions of symbolic rivers in Ezekiel 47 and Revelation
22.

The Tigris and Euphrates Rivers relate Eden to geography as we
know it. These rivers, which flow through Mesopotamia, have their
sources in the north among the mountains of Armenia. It is evident
that the writer of Genesis was describing northern Mesopotamia as
the geographic location of the cradle of creation and human history.

Mankind's moral requirement (2:15–17).—The presence in the garden of the tree of the knowledge of good and evil established a moral
demand that rests upon humanity. God placed man in the garden
and gave him the task of keeping it. Work was assigned, not as a
curse of sin—for no sin had yet entered the picture—but as a part
of God's plan for human life. Mankind had from the beginning both
the capacity and responsibility to share with God in the ongoing creative development and utilization of the resources of the world.

As mankind lived out this planned partnership with God, provisions
were made for people to enjoy a full and pleasant life. The first man
was told to eat freely of all the trees of the garden except the tree
of knowledge of good and evil. The trees of this garden had already
been described as "pleasant to the sight and good for food" (v. 9).
It was in regard to the tree of knowledge, however, that the concern
of moral requirement arose. Of that tree the man was commanded
not to eat. His willingness to obey was on trial and the outcome of
his life was at stake, for God warned that if he should eat of that
tree he would die.

The twofold nature of death is important for understanding this passage. The nature of the death experience is essentially one of separation. There is an experience called death that is physical. This is the event when the spiritual dimension of human life, along with the physical life, is separated from the body and the body disintegrates through decay. There is also an experience called death that is spiritual. This is the state of relationship with God in which a person is alienated from God through disobedience, rebellion, trespasses, and sins (see Eph. 2:1).

The moral dimension of the Garden of Eden experience indicates that the death which would result from disobedience was spiritual death—that is, alienation from God. Human vulnerability, physical death, and the length of human physical life may have been involved; but the primary meaning of death was disharmony and broken fellowship with God. This was demonstrated later by the writer's description of the fall of man into sin.

What was the nature of the moral requirement placed upon mankind? It is described as obedience to God's command concerning the tree of the knowledge of good and evil. The basic meaning involves living with the responsibility of moral choice rather than living as a creature of instinct. Human persons have the capacity to choose the quality of their response to God. They can choose to obey or disobey, thus to do good or to do evil. Eating from the tree of the knowledge of good and evil had to do with how people would handle their capacity of moral choice in their living relationship with God. Indeed, obedience was on trial and destiny was at stake.

Need for companionship (2:18-24).—The creation of woman as companion for man reveals something significant about the nature of human persons. They are social beings. Few people have any disposition to be "loners." Times of solitude are helpful for looking inward and reflecting upon life, but association with others is vitally important for the full development of personhood. The biblical statement "It is not good that the man should be alone" (v. 18) reveals the human need for companionship.

Because people share their nature of personhood with God, this also reveals something about his nature. Instead of living in majestic aloneness, God created the world. Instead of making all creation subject to his absolute control, God created human persons who could respond to him, out of the free choice of their own moral nature, in obedience or disobedience. The fact that God created people with the capacity for personal fellowship reveals his desire for sharing in such fellowship, rather than existing in isolated solitariness. This quality in the character of God is also reflected in the threefold but unified nature of God as Father, Son, and Holy Spirit, which is revealed in the New Testament.

Mankind was created to have a need for companionship—a need that could be fulfilled only by other human persons, not by association with animals. This insight is revealed in the creation of a woman, who was to be a companion for man. But persons need companionship with other persons. This is the significance of the statement that man found in woman one who was "bone of my bones, and flesh of my flesh" (v. 23). Man and woman, though created sexually different as male and female, are nevertheless of the same human species. They correspond to each other in human personhood and have the capacity to complement each other through companionship.

This passage of Scripture provides amazing insight into the relationship between man and woman. The worth of woman is held at a high level. She was valued for herself. No emphasis was made on her child-bearing role; so she was not to be valued as a man's reproductive extension of himself. Coming, as this does, out of an ancient patriarchal culture which did not hold a high view of woman, the passage reveals a distinctive quality of divine inspiration. The beauty of sexuality is affirmed in that there was no sense of shame in their being naked. The unique excellence of marriage is revealed, for it provides the intimate relationship in which human companionship reaches fullest fruition.

So the message which the writer was setting forth is that in the human species, and in human family life, there is found the central focus of life on earth. God had created mankind to have an exalted place in the world. Man's relation to his Creator has been the continuing basis of the Hebrew-Christian religion.

Making Itself the Center of Its World (3:1-24)

The scene was set for the first great moral drama in the history of the world. Man and woman were living in mutually fulfilling companionship with each other and in fellowship with God. Their environment in Eden provided pleasant surroundings and amply supplied

their needs. What happened to that good creation and to man's fellowship with his Creator? Why the difference between that ideal world
and the world that people have known through the ages? Why is
there so much evil and violence in the world? Answers to these questions are found in the account of the fall of mankind into sin, a record
that sets forth the tragic truth that from the beginning human persons
have been in revolt against the sovereignty of God.

Enter temptation (3:1–6).—The presence of moral temptation in
human life is illustrated by the introduction of a crafty tempter. The
tempter picked up on a command that God had given to the man
and woman, and with it he challenged the requirement that God
had made. He also cast doubt upon the relationship on which that
requirement was based. The tempter distorted the things God had
commanded by asking, "Did God [really] say, 'You shall not eat of
any tree in the garden'?" (v. 1).

The effect of that question was to make an insinuation against God,
to cast doubt on his motives, and to arouse suspicion in the mind of
the woman. After all, should God withhold anything good from the
people he had created? Was God being selfish in not wanting to share
the knowledge of good and evil with them?

The woman corrected the tempter by pointing out that only the
tree of the knowledge of good and evil was denied to them, while
they were permitted to eat freely of all the other trees. And God's
reason for restricting the one tree was to keep them from harm; if
they were to eat of it they would die.

Then the tempter made his supreme move. He dared to contradict
God and used a bold falsehood to persuade the woman to disregard
God's warning and disobey his command. He said, "You will not
die, . . . you will be like God" (vv. 4–5). The subtle hint behind the
tempter's statement was that the relationship with God would not
really be damaged, for people who had broader moral experiences
could have a better relationship with God. It was such a beautiful
temptation. The idea was so plausible. The only trouble was that it
was not true.

So far, the course of the temptation experience had been: a question
by the tempter, a correcting reply by the woman, and a deceiving
suggestion by the tempter. Then the "tempter" inside took over, and
the woman persuaded herself that the tree was "desired to make
one wise" (v. 6). Here is illustrated the truth of Jesus' words "For

from within, out of the heart of man, come evil thoughts" (Mark 7:21). Here is illustrated the wisdom of the counsel in Proverbs 4:23, "Keep your heart with all vigilance; for from it flow the springs of life." Conscience said, "Obey God." Temptation said, "Look how pleasant and desirable the way of disobedience is." The heart of the woman took the side of the temptation and invited her husband to join her in it. Both of them chose the way of disobedience and sin.

Something new on the scene—sin (3:6-7).—With their choice of disobedience, the people became sinful. Because of their moral nature, sin was possible. By their disobedient action, sin became actual. With it came the resulting guilt and alienation from God. Their sense of personal guilt created in them a sense of shame about who they were. Their nakedness, which had created no shame in their earlier moral innocence, now became a source of shame. They made some garments of leaves to cover themselves in an attempt to relieve the painful sense of shame that had come to them.

The nature of that event, by which the people became sinful, was disobedient rebellion against their relationship with God. The true nature of the divine-human relationship was one in which the Creator was sovereign and the creature was subordinate. That kind of relationship would belong inherently to any Creator-creature relationship. But those creatures, the man and the woman, attempted to escape from their subordinate position and to extend their control over their lives beyond the bounds for humanity that God as Creator had established.

Those human persons had become convinced that they would be better off as autonomous individuals than as creatures living in subordinate obedience to God. So they attempted to seize what did not belong to them and to usurp the moral prerogative that belonged to God. They took a flight into a foolish fantasy, imagining that they were as wise as God about what is good and evil.

The relationship between God and mankind thus became tragically and sinfully disordered. Their disobedience had its roots in their pride. They thought of themselves more highly than they ought to think (see Rom. 12:3). The essence of their sin was egotism. They chose to make themselves the center of their world.

Something new had been added to the human scene. It was human sinfulness. They had done what the tempter suggested. They had disobeyed God by declaring their independence from him. Their declaration did not make them independent, however. Their rebellion against subordination to God did not nullify his sovereignty or make them autonomous beings. And the experience did not turn out as the tempter had said it would. He had promised them falsely that they would become like God, knowing good and evil. All they learned from the experience was what it means to be disobedient, guilty, full of shame, and alienated from God. Those were the consequences of human sinfulness.

Alienation—a discordant relationship (3:8-10).—God and people were still in the same world, just as they had been before the human turn into sinfulness. God was still sovereign. The people were still dependent creatures. They were still inevitably related to each other, but that relationship had been changed radically. A moral chasm had been created. Disharmony had replaced accord. Alienation had replaced fellowship.

Because God desires fellowship, he came seeking the man and the woman. His question "Where are you?" (v. 9) speaks with singular application to all people in all ages as well as to those first sinful people. God's presence stirred feelings of guilt. His probing question called forth an expression of fear and shame. The resulting interchange led to the crucial question, "Have you eaten of the tree of which I commanded you not to eat?" (v. 11). Apparently, the man and woman realized that denial would have been futile. They found themselves trapped in a relationship where moral guilt had breached the harmony of their fellowship with God. They could not get away from God or themselves.

Alibis—an attempt to evade responsibility (3:11-13).—What do you do when you are caught red-handed? You can confess, deny, or try to find a way to clear yourself of blame. With God, denial would have been futile. The deep sense of guilt made confession too painful. So the man first, and then the woman, took the route of alibi, seeking to justify themselves by placing the blame on someone else.

The man used a double alibi. He stated that the woman was at fault because she gave him the fruit, as though no course of action was open to him except to eat it. He even implied that God was responsible, since God had made the woman who offered him the forbidden fruit. Thus, he raised a moral question for every age. Is God responsible for sin because he created a human situation in which temptation and sin are possible? Are forces outside us responsible for our sinfulness, and are we consequently freed from personal responsibility?

God's answers to the man and woman there at the beginning of human history settled that moral question for all times. No ideal environment will keep people from sin. Nor can the moral guilt of sinfulness be evaded by placing responsibility on some other person or outside influence. When the first couple tried to use alibis for what they had done, God would not let them play games with themselves or with him. The man blamed the woman and God, and the woman blamed the tempter; but the serpent was not even permitted a reply. The experience of guilt and alienation, which had come because of sinfulness, had come through the people's own choice and action. They could not evade their personal responsibility.

God's edict of consequences (3:14–19).—Sin has within itself the seeds of its consequential punishment. God spoke of the consequences of their sinful rebellion to each in turn—to the serpent, the woman, and the man. This edict as recorded may have been a very ancient Hebrew poem and part of the inspired oral heritage that the writer used in compiling the record of human origins in Genesis. It describes in graphic language the sad results of a human choice of rebellion and sin.

The curse upon the serpent explained why snakes have no legs, why they crawl as they do, and why people have such a fear and revulsion toward serpents of all kinds. It also gives an explanation of the idea, incorrectly believed by ancient people, that snakes live on dust as their food.

Into the curse upon the serpent there is also set a statement of promise and hope. The edict of enmity between mankind and serpents anticipated the agelong struggle between good and evil. But the promise "he shall bruise your head" (v. 15) is an expression of assurance of the ultimate triumph of good over evil. The promise probably should not be called messianic, but this hope of victory over evil is certainly the seedbed out of which the Hebrew messianic hope developed. Jesus Christ achieved through incarnation the very victory of which this promise speaks.

No curse was spoken upon either the woman or the man. Because of their turning into sinfulness, they had become victims of the consequences of the sin they had chosen. God's edict was a declaration that they would reap the results of their participation in evil. The judgment declared upon the woman explained to the ancients why human reproduction involves pain and why women were held in a subordinate role to men in patriarchal cultures. The judgment declared upon the man explained to the ancients why work involves burdensome toil and why the universe, which was created good, had become so "unfriendly." Since work was a part of the intentional plan for man before the fall into sin (2:15), work itself is not a curse because of sin.

The consequence of sin is described as toil and sweat in an environment of thorns and thistles, instead of work in the pleasant garden where the man and woman had lived before their sin. These consequences of sin were declared by God to be the circumstances of life for people until the end of their physical lives. These circumstances would prevail until "you return to the ground, for out of it you were taken; you are dust and to dust you shall return" (v. 19). This was to be the course of life for all until the natural end of life.

The consequence of sin was not a loss of the germ of immortality, so that people became subject to physical death. The mortality of physical death was to be the natural end of life because of the created nature of human life. The early human drama recorded in Genesis does not indicate that sinfulness brought upon mankind a vulnerability to physical death that was not present before they turned to sin. What happened in the sin experience was a spiritual alienation from fellowship with God. In that sense when the man and the woman sinned, they surely did die.

The many varied troubles of life are declared to be a part of the consequences of human sinfulness, and these troubles will continue to be the condition within which life is lived until it reaches its natural end in physical death. This was the edict God issued to mankind as he began to deal with their sinfulness and with the disharmony in the relation between them and himself.

Renewed affirmation of life (3:20–24).—The people were able to hear God's promise of an ultimate victory over evil, however. They were able also to make a new affirmation of the goodness of life, even though it was now blighted by the consequences of sinfulness. The man gave his wife a name. He called her Eve, a name which means "living"; and thus he declared that life goes on and is fruitful.

God also gave a new affirmation of the worth of life by a twofold gift of grace. First, he provided garments of animal skins to clothe them. In that way God showed that he would not use their shame in a vindictive way to make them suffer for their disobedience. Rather, he would help them overcome the reasons for their shame. The Creator who had been sinned against took the initiative to begin a redemptive work among the very people who had sinned against him. This redemptive love of God came to fullest measure when Jesus died on Calvary for sinners.

God expressed his loving concern for the fallen man and woman by sending them out of the garden. On first consideration, this appears to be a punishment for disobedience. But upon closer study, it stands clearly as an evidence that God was dealing with them in a redemptive way. Notice the reason God gave for sending them from the garden— "Lest he put forth his hand and take also of the tree of life, and eat, and live forever" (v. 22). Nothing worse could happen to the person than to be sealed forever in a life of rebellion against God, and that is exactly the condition in which the people were at that time. Nothing could be more loving than to seek redemption of sinners before they "eat of the tree of life and live forever." So God removed them from the garden and sealed it.

His next work would be an age of redemption to bring mankind back to restored fellowship with himself through his saving grace. The human family had tried to make themselves the center of the world through sinful rebellion against God. God gave a new affirmation of the worth of those sinful persons by initiating an age of redemption. This has been the subsequent story of his dealing with humanity.

Reaping the Continued Consequences of Evil (4:1–24)

After recording the removal of the first sinful persons from the garden, the writer of Genesis turned to a description of the development of human society outside the garden. The family of mankind expanded and spread across the earth. That development is described as having been from one family; and the writer began to use personal names instead of the generic descriptions "the man" and "the woman," which were used in the earlier stories.

First children born (4:1–2).—Cain and Abel were born to Adam and Eve. This is the first record of the phenomenon of human birth. The subject of reproduction is dealt with in an open but discreet way. The process of sexual intercourse is referred to by the expression "Adam *knew* Eve his wife" (v. 1). That manner of speaking about sexual intercourse reflects a profound insight into the complex intimacy involved in copulation.

Cain was the firstborn. His name was based on a Hebrew root word meaning to get. Eve responded to his birth by saying, "I have *gotten* a man with the help of the Lord" (v. 1). Evidently that was an expression of celebration. To them a sense of miracle had occurred, since the birth of a human child had never happened before. To reproduce gave them a proud sense of accomplishment.

The second child was named Abel. No indication is given in the text of the significance of his name. The root word from which the name Abel came means a breath or a vapor. The name could have been chosen by his parents to express their feeling that he was as intimately close and precious to them as their very breath. Looking back as we do upon the events that followed, his name was something of an omen of the briefness of his life.

Cain grew up to be a farmer like his father, but Abel became a shepherd. Their life-styles were thus different, and in those differences they represented the conflict of cultures between agricultural and pastoral people that has prevailed through the ages. Historically, these groups have each thought their life-style more excellent and their products more valuable than the other. No such distinctions of work are valid, however. In anticipation of their settling in Palestine, Moses reminded the people that the land was "a land of wheat and barley, of vines and fig trees"; but it was also a land where their "flocks and herds" would multiply (Deut. 8:8,13). In the broad spectrum of human society, there is a place for both farmers and herdsmen; and both in significant ways are dependent upon each other.

Personal conflict arose (4:3-7).—Cain and Abel made offerings of their products to the Lord. Their offerings were apparently expressions of thanksgiving, though no statement about their meaning is given. The writer made no explanation of them, evidently because sacrificial offerings were such a common feature in the life of his time. There is no hint that these offerings by Cain and Abel were made for confession and forgiveness of sin.

Cain's offering most likely was one of fruit or grain, while Abel offered a lamb from the flock. Abel's offering was received by God with approval, but Cain's was not. The difference in their acceptability to God did not rest on the fact that one was an animal sacrifice and the other was from plants. Both plant and animal offerings were acceptable to God (see Ex. 32:29–30). Since no reason is given for Cain's offering being unacceptable, we can only surmise that it was because Cain himself was unacceptable to God due to his attitude or lack of faith. Abel was later described as having offered a more acceptable sacrifice by faith (Heb. 11:4). An indication of this meaning is found in the emphasis of the order used by the writer. God approved *Abel and* his offering, but not *Cain and* his offering.

So Cain's offering was rejected because Cain was rejected. For some reason he was out of fellowship with God. His reaction provides a clue to what the trouble may have been. Cain became very angry over what had happened. He was obviously jealous that Abel had received God's favor and he had not. It is interesting to note that the trouble between Cain and Abel arose over a religious issue. It is a quite common human trait for people who do not measure up in moral excellence themselves to have hostile feelings toward those who do.

God warned Cain about the possible consequences of his resentful reaction to the experience of having his offering rejected. The clear indication was that if Cain would get straightened out himself, he and his offering would both be accepted. But sinfulness constituted an ever-present jeopardy to Cain, just as it does to everyone. The description of sin "*couching* at the door" (v. 7) is the figure of an animal crouching beside a door ready to spring upon anyone who passes through it. God's warning to Cain was that sin is always ready to rise up in the form of jealousy or anger, to take over a person's life, and to dominate his actions. But Cain would not listen to God; nor would he quell his jealous anger toward his brother.

Anger broke out into violence (4:8–10).—Cain killed his brother Abel, and the first murder in human society occurred. But was this murder? Did Cain intentionally plan to destroy his brother's life out of jealousy and hatred? Since no human death had ever taken place, did Cain understand what the result of his violence might be? Animals had been killed, however, so Cain evidently knew the meaning of death. He certainly seems to have planned some violence against Abel, for he set the stage and carefully chose the time and place. Crime has always shunned observation. Cain got Abel out into the field, away from their parents, and there killed him. Yes, it was murder.

But God was there. He put Cain on trial with the questions: "Where is your brother?" and "What have you done?" Cain responded with defiance and falsehood. He showed contempt for God, as though God had no right to ask. He told an outright lie in declaring he did not know where his brother was. He denied that the whole matter was any concern of his by the insolent question "Am I my brother's keeper?"

One sin, jealousy, had led to a second sin, murder—which in turn had led to a third sin, lying. Sin does spring up, get control of life, alienate one from God, and corrupt human relations. God's unheeded warning had come to pass. Cain had not mastered evil (4:7); so evil had mastered him.

The consequences of evil are harsh (4:11–16).—God told Cain what the consequences of his evil would be. The judgment was not stated as an arbitrary penalty of punishment. The curse was not God's retaliation against Cain. It was the inherent consequence of Cain's violation of God's moral laws.

Since Cain had shed his brother's blood upon the ground, the ground itself would repudiate him. No longer would the earth yield its fruit to him. No longer would there be any spot of land upon the earth that would own him and be his. He would henceforth be a fugitive and wanderer with no homeland.

By his sin Cain had further separated himself from the favor of God, which he had so jealously envied when his brother received it. He had deepened the tragedy of his condition by making himself repulsive to the created world also. He cried out in anguish that he could not stand such complete rejection: "My punishment is greater than I can bear" (v. 13). To have no acceptance with God or the world would mean having no identity and no security. He would be vulnerable to being killed by anyone he met, and nobody would care or come to his aid. It is necessary here to assume some passage of time with an increase of population in the world, for the sense of danger expressed was broader than any possible retaliation by Adam and Eve.

God responded with an expression of grace. He declared that Cain was not to be subject to perpetual vengeance. God put a mark upon Cain to identify him as being under God's protection. There is no indication of the nature of that "mark of Cain," but it is clear that it was not to be an instrument of shame and disgrace. The mark was a provision of God enabling Cain to find redemption and rebuild his life rather than be destroyed by sin.

So Cain went out to live in the land of Nod. It is vaguely described as being "east of Eden" (v. 16), but its geography is completely unknown. The name Nod means wandering and quite likely was not intended to describe an area of land. Cain became a fugitive wanderer. He was the original "man without a country."

Cain's descendants (4:17–24).—The writer included a summary record of Cain's clan to complete the account of his history. After such a summary the line of Cain would be left, and the line of Seth followed as it carried forward the story of God's work in the world.

These summary verses reflect a long passage of time with significant development of human civilization. It is obvious that the writer was not attempting to include all the details of human history. His purpose was to write the moral and spiritual history of mankind's relation to God. So in a sweeping summary, the contributions of Cain's progeny to the developing culture of humanity are recorded.

Cain himself built a city and named it after his son Enoch. This Enoch should not be confused with the Enoch of the Seth line, whose walk with God is recorded in Genesis 5:24. The building of a city necessarily implies the presence of a large population.

Six generations later Cain's descendants are described as being the heads of three branches of art and vocation. Jabal was the father of the nomadic herdsmen; Jubal of the musicians; and Tubal-Cain of the metal craftsmen. Human civilization was developing. The things of culture that people were developing could be and have been used for both good and evil, for both noble and ignoble purposes. The people of the world were fulfilling the original command to subdue the earth and have dominion over it (see 1:28), but there is a moral dimension to that dominion. And the moral struggle of human civilization has continued through every age.

The course of human history has lain under the shadow of sin; and while there has been advance in culture and civilization, there have often been tragic declines in morality. Lamech was one of the sad examples of that truth. He was the first recorded bigamist, disregarding the ideal of monogamy in marriage. His harsh cruelty, however, is a more tragic illustration of his moral perversion. He proudly

called attention to the fact that he had killed men for injuring him
and even for striking him (v. 23). He declared that he would take
tenfold more vengeance on anyone injuring him than God had set
forth for any violence against Cain. The law of exact retribution, which
limited retaliation to *only* an eye for an eye and a tooth for a tooth,
was kindness in comparison to Lamech's cruelty.

With the summary of Cain's life and descendants, the writer completed a major section of his recording of human history. Humanity
had been given the unique place at the apogee of all creation, but
moral failure had come quickly to these creatures who were created
in the image of God. While they had been made to have dominion
within creation, the earliest people chose to rebel against the superior
dominion of the Creator. Human history became characterized by
alienation from God and disorder within human relations. Violence
and death became a part of the human scene. After the first four
chapters of Genesis, a new direction was taken by the writer. He
set out to describe how God dealt with sinful humanity in ways to
bring redemption and call out a covenant people. The birth of Seth
was the introduction of that story.

Notes

1. Gerhard von Rad, *Genesis* (Philadelphia: The Westminster Press, 1971),
p. 66.
2. William Barclay, *Letters of James and Peter* (Philadelphia: The Westminster Press, 1960), p. 109.

God and Humanity
4:25 to 11:32

Cain and his descendants turned to evil, and the taint of evil that
had infected them left little hope for humanity. But the writer of
Genesis knew that God does not give up easily. In the story of the
birth of Seth, there is a record of how a new beginning was made.

Since the line of the faithful was to be found in the descendants of
Seth, the focus of Genesis followed the development of that family
line.

Grace and Hope (4:25 to 5:32)

When Seth was born he was given his name, which means "appointed." That choice of name for the newborn reflected the parents'
faith that God had not forsaken them. He had given them a child
who was appointed to fill the void in the family left by the death of
Abel and the self-exile of Cain. Evil had brought terrible tragedy
into their lives, but they were not cast down into hopeless despair.
God had shown his grace by giving them another son, and through
that son they had new hope.

A significant facet of Hebrew history is reflected in the beginning
of the story of Seth and his descendants. A distinction was made between one family of people which had a special relationship with
God and the other family lines which did not. At that early point in
human history there began to be made a distinction between the
covenant people of God and all other nations, and that distinction
grew in importance to the Hebrews through the centuries.

The beginning of worship (4:26).—As the family of Seth developed,
they began to practice worship. While the offerings of Cain and Abel
(4:3-4) were an elementary form of religious expression, only at this
later time did developed worship become an established part of human life.

Sin had caused alienation between people and God. The conflicts
of personal and cultural differences had caused friction, violence, and
separation within the human family. Those deep divisions had made
alienation the very soil of the social and spiritual environment in
which people lived. The development of worship opened a way for
reconciliation to take place. The hand of God, moving in grace, was
evident as he inspired people to follow his leading into the way of
good life.

In these passages about early human events the name Yahweh is
used in the Hebrew to refer to God (chaps. 2—4). Yahweh is identified
as the God Seth and his family worshiped, but we are not sure that
they knew and used this personal name for God. No explanation of

the meaning or significance of the name is given in any of these
Genesis passages. Notice that the name is used in statements of narrative description by the writer of Genesis as he recorded God's involve-
ment with humanity. Use of the personal name of God by the people
at this early stage of human history would be in contrast to the passage
in Exodus that indicates that the Hebrews first knew God as Yahweh
when he revealed himself to Moses (Ex. 3:4). Using the name to describe the Seth family's worship probably affirms that they were worshiping the true God. It was Yahweh they worshiped, even if they
did not know him by that name.

From creation to flood (5:1-32).—The theme of grace and hope
is reflected in the genealogy that spans the human scene from the
beginning to the flood. This record of the family line from Adam to
Noah accounts for their direct kinship through Seth and his descendants, instead of through Cain or another of Adam's children. The
purpose of Genesis is clearly to show that Israel's history was not a
result of human accident. It was shaped by God as he found and
chose a faithful line of people with whom he could make a lasting
covenant of fellowship.

This family record of the Seth line from Adam to Noah is one of
the ten genealogies in Genesis that mark transitions from one major
period of development to another. Focus on the exalted creation of
mankind was renewed with the declaration that God made man in
his likeness. Through the miracle of human birth, people share in
the perpetuation of their superior position within creation. Having
been made in the likeness of God, Adam "became the father of a
son in his own likeness" (5:3). In human personhood, the "image of
God" has been continued from generation to generation since the
beginning.

A specific formula was used by the writer for each person included
in this list of Seth's descendants. First he recorded the age of the
person at the time of the birth of the descendant through whom
the family heritage would be traced. Then recognition was given to
the rest of the family by recording that there were other sons and
daughters. Each person's record was closed with a record of his total
years of life and the fact of his death (with the exception of Enoch
and Noah).

The recorded length of life in this period of human history creates
some problem for understanding and interpretation. The life span

for the period from Adam to Noah was said to be 700 to 1,000 years. From Noah to Abraham, the ages were generally recorded to be from 200 to 600 years, though it is indicated in Genesis 6:3 that 120 years was to be the normal length of life. The Hebrew patriarchs are described as having lived from 100 to 200 years. And the psalmist wrote of an average life span of 70 to 80 years (90:10). Was this radical shortening of life span due to the effects of sin? Did the ancient people use different units of time for measuring the length of life? We simply have no way of knowing.

The story of Enoch's life is essentially the same as that of others in this family record. His story has one unusual feature, however, in that "Enoch walked with God, and he was not, for God took him" (v. 24). The verse as it stands does not necessarily imply that he escaped physical death. Hebrews 11:5 indicates, however, a clear tradition that he did not die a physical death but was supernaturally translated into the spiritual world.

Enoch was a distinctive person. His exemplary life of fellowship with God made him spiritually outstanding. Evidently, the quality of his personal devotion to God made the line of demarcation between the physical and spiritual worlds practically indistinguishable. In the midst of a genealogy that includes the recurring refrain of death, Enoch's translation brings into focus the hope of overcoming death. Death is a normal part of human life. Physical life ends in physical death. But people are created in the image of God and have a distinctive spiritual dimension to life. Like Enoch, by living in fellowship with God, others can overcome death. Authentic fellowship with God will not be destroyed by the ending of physical life. Grace makes hope real.

The introduction of Noah (5:28–32).—At the end of this series of descendants in the Adam/Seth family line, Noah is introduced. That completes the transition the writer was making from the creation narrative to the events of the great flood. The lineage record was left open-ended, for the story being recorded was that of the ongoing history of God and humanity—sometimes in fellowship and sometimes in conflict.

Noah's name means deliverer. The root word on which the name is built can have variety in meaning: to deliver, to cause to rest, to cause to settle down. At least three facets of meaning relate Noah's name to his role in human history. (1) His father, Lamech, is described as holding great hope that Noah would be the "deliverer" who would provide the secrets of agriculture by which the hard toil of farming could be relieved (5:29). (2) Following the flood Noah is described as a farmer (9:20), so we can assume he was a farmer before the flood as well. As the first primary developer of agriculture as a vocation, Noah would "cause the people to settle down" and cultivate the land. Then the nomadic life of wandering herdsmen would no longer be necessary to find grazing and provide food. (3) Of course, as the builder of the ark, Noah was a great deliverer who preserved human and animal life through the disastrous flood.

Judgment and Redemption (6:1 to 9:17)

The story of God's dealing with humanity not only contains the indications of grace and hope. The question of judgment or redemption was necessary because of human sinfulness. That question is dealt with in the story of the great flood. But before developing that ongoing story, the writer included a digression to explain that superior men were not the answer to the problem of evil and death in the human situation.

A parenthesis about giants (6:1–4).—This passage reveals a primitive tradition that a race of giants, the Nephilim (6:4; Num. 13:33), were the offspring of mating between some divine beings and human women. This semidivine ancestry was believed to account for their greater-than-normal size, strength, and prowess.

The presence of such people within the human race raised a question of the future of mankind. Would a superrace develop which would eventually overcome death and finally achieve immortality? That question was answered by this passage in Genesis. The answer was no. The problem of human mortality would not be solved by the development of a giant people who would be strong enough to win the battle with death.

Even the most superior people are only human; consequently, they are subject to the mortal limits of life just as are all other people. An average life span of 120 years (6:3) was evidently intended to apply to the giants as well as to other people.

No indication is included in the passage that there was any moral wrong involved. Nor is it indicated that this event was directly linked to the coming judgment of the flood. The great evil described in the following passage was characteristic of all the people, not just the giants. So it does seem that this passage is a true parenthesis. The writer does not present the development of giants as a result of what had gone before or as a cause of what was to come afterward.

Universal wickedness of mankind (6:5–8).—In these verses the writer gave his introduction to the entire flood narrative that was to follow. The meaning of the flood was revealed. It was an expression of divine judgment upon the widespread evil in the world.

Thorough corruptness had developed within humanity. "The wickedness of man was great," and "every imagination of the thoughts of his heart was only evil continually" (v. 5). Where was the hope for humanity that had been reflected in the beginning of the Seth line to replace the corrupt clan of Cain? Sin had taken over the whole of humanity to the extent that there was no hope that mankind could recover to righteousness.

The universal evil in mankind confronted God with a divine dilemma. What would he do in the face of such complete human sinfulness? God was grieved to his heart about the condition that had developed. Had God really created beings who could not handle the moral capacities that had been given to them? Was there any way to correct the situation? Or was the only solution to eliminate humanity and start over? Is there a breaking point when decency can no longer hold back the deluge of evil consequences that come from sin? The writer of Genesis recorded a divine decision to eliminate all human creatures. That decision was not made in cold indifference by an unfeeling God, however. He cared; he agonized; he was hurt to the heart by the evil that called for his righteous judgment.

God wrestled with the question of judgment or redemption. He had decided on judgment and destruction—but then there was Noah, a man of integrity. So the text indicates that the decision of judgment was modified to include both destruction and redemption. Life on the earth would be destroyed, but Noah and his family would be spared. The condition of mankind was not totally hopeless. The flood was not a complete cancellation of God's purpose in his creation of life in the world.

Preparation for the flood (6:9–22).—Noah was a man who had integrity in his own personal character, in his relationship with his fellowman, and in his relationship with God. His life illustrates how important one person can be whose life is genuinely in touch with God. Fellowship with God enabled him to see the way God was leading and to follow him.

The story of the flood opens with a restatement of God's judgment upon human evil (vv. 11–12). In his instructions to Noah, God revealed his plan to preserve a specimen remnant of all animal life to repopulate the earth after the flood. Note that the flood narrative is third person throughout. There is no record of Noah speaking until after the flood (see 9:24–27).

Noah was led by God to build an ark of gopher wood (probably a species of cypress) and seal it with pitch (a bituminous tar). Its size was to be 450 feet long, 75 feet wide, and 45 feet high. Those dimensions would make it about half the size of a modern ocean liner. Its displacement would be something over 40,000 tons. Its construction was a great achievement for that ancient day. The ark had three decks to provide living space for the animals and storage space for the food that would be needed. It was covered with a roof to shed the rains that would fall. There were no sails or other means of movement. The ark would merely float and drift.

A covenant was promised to Noah, to his sons, and to the representative animals (6:18). God's covenant with Noah was a covenant of deliverance in the face of divine judgment upon evil. This was a conditional covenant. God would preserve their lives only if Noah would trust God enough to build the ark, and only if they would all obey God and take refuge in the ark when the flood came.

The story of the flood (7:1 to 8:22).—God commanded Noah to enter the ark that he had earlier instructed him to build. At that point a new element was introduced into the story. Noah was told to take into the ark with him seven pairs of each clean animal but only one pair of each unclean animal. This was in contrast to an earlier commandment to take with him a single pair of all living species (6:19). No indication is given whether the cleanness and uncleanness referred to their use for food or their use for sacrifice. After the flood Noah offered burnt offerings of every clean animal and bird (8:20). We can assume that the need for clean animals for food and sacrifice was the reason for larger numbers of those being saved.

Then the rains began to fall and floodwaters began to rise. Ancient peoples believed that rains came from a great ocean of water above the sky. Springs were believed to flow out from a great ocean under the earth. The great flood is described as resulting from both these oceans breaking forth to pour their waters upon the face of the earth (7:11). The floodwaters rose until life on the face of the known world was destroyed except for that which was preserved in the ark (7:18–21).

A beautiful description of grace is reflected in the statement that "God remembered Noah and all the beasts and the cattle that were with him in the ark" (8:1). God watched over the ark with loving care. He brought an end to the deluge, and as the waters receded "the ark came to rest upon the mountains of Ararat" (8:4). The Ararat mountains are in the land of Armenia. Assuming that Noah had lived somewhere in the area of Mesopotamia, the ark had drifted hundreds of miles to the northwest.

As the waters continued to recede, the tops of the mountains became visible again. Noah began to test for a time when they could leave the ark. He sent out a raven that did not return. He sent out a dove that returned first with nothing, but a week later with an olive leaf in its mouth. This was an indication to Noah that the lower lands were clear, for olive trees do not grow at very high elevations. After another week he sent the dove out again, and she did not return. So after a full year and ten days (compare 7:11 and 8:13–14) Noah opened the ark, and they all came out on the earth again.

Noah's first action was to build an altar and offer sacrifices of gratitude to God. In return he received two promises from God: (1) God would never again destroy life on earth because of evil, and (2) the seasons would continue dependably and without fail. Note that these were unconditional promises. Nothing was required of those rescued people for the promises to become effective. God made some very important promises, and those promises have been cherished through all the ages since. They are a clear revelation that God is in the orderly events as well as in the catastrophic. He is active in providence as well as in judgment. The inspired truth that God is the giver of seedtime and harvest was a great message for the later day of the final writer of Genesis when Baal influence was so strong in Palestine. (Baal was believed by the pagan Canaanites to be the agricultural god who blessed the fields with fertility and rain.)

A note about flood stories.—There are many traditions about great floods that arose at many places among different peoples. One, called the Gilgamish epic, parallels the story of the Bible most closely. The

Gilgamish epic was known in Mesopotamia as early as 3000 B.C., and the writer of Genesis may well have been familiar with it. The biblical record of the great flood is superior to other flood stories, however, and reflects a true quality of inspiration. The strong monotheism and the high moral purpose revealed in the Genesis account of the flood puts that narrative into a class by itself in which it has no close parallel.

A new beginning (9:1-17).—Having been delivered from judgment, Noah represents redeemed humanity. He was commanded to make a new start. The instruction to "be fruitful and multiply, and fill the earth" (9:1) is almost identical to the command given to humanity at the first creation (1:28). It was apparently God's intention that organized life should emerge and develop as it had from the first chaos (1:2-31).

Death and violence were recognized as part of the pattern of life on earth. The dominion of mankind over other animals was renewed, but the sacredness of life was clearly affirmed. While animals were to be used for food, blood was not to be eaten. This prohibition against eating blood was based on the conviction that "the life of the flesh is in the blood" (Lev. 17:11).

The special sacredness of human life was established in the ban that was placed against shedding human blood (9:6). Since man is created in the image of God and since man's life was believed to be centered in his blood, then human blood has a very special sacredness and must not be shed.

A requirement of blood for blood shed was an establishment of order to prevent anarchy or excessive vengeance as Cain and Lamech had done (4:5-8,23-24). Order is necessary to protect sacredness of life and to restrain the evil that results from human sin.

In the new beginning, God made the covenant with Noah as he had promised (6:18; 9:9). God would not destroy the earth by water again. This was a universal covenant with Noah and his descendants, as well as with the animals of the earth. It was an unconditional covenant: God made the promise without requiring anything of mankind in return. And he gave people a sign of that covenant to assure them of the promise he had made.

God used the rainbow as a covenant sign. The bow was an ancient weapon of war and symbolized suffering and tyranny. But God used a rainbow, a bow laid down, to symbolize peace. Judgment was passed.

Hope and redemption were God's gracious purposes for his relation to mankind.

People today know something of the principle of light refraction by which rainbows are made visible. But light refraction and rainbows are not accidents. God made the principles of natural law by which rainbows occur, and he used the rainbow to assure Noah that rain would not always mean flood. Without that assurance people would have lived in fear that every rain might be the beginning of another deluge on the earth.

God had made a new beginning by sending people forth to populate the earth and build human civilization to fulfill God's original purpose in creation. He gave mankind the hope of his sure promise of gracious care to undergird them. Would the moral situation among humanity be any better after the flood judgment than it had been before? A story of tragic sadness would unfold.

Continuing Disharmony (9:18 to 11:32)

The new beginning that followed the flood revolved around Noah, his three sons, and their families. Those persons who had been spared from death in the deluge were the nucleus of a new humanity. For some unstated reason, Canaan was included as the fifth person named in the first recorded event following the flood. He is identified as a son of Ham and a grandson of Noah.

Noah: the vine grower (9:18–23).—Though Noah was described before the flood as a righteous and blameless man, it did not take long after the flood for the evil consequences of sin to surface within his family. Noah is called "the first tiller of the soil" (9:20), but earlier Cain had also been called "a tiller of the ground" (4:2). Evidently Noah originated a new agricultural occupation, the planting and cultivating of vines.

The location of their residence here clearly seems to be back in the fertile valley of Mesopotamia. Noah had evidently migrated southeastward from Ararat and settled again near the place where he had lived before the flood.

As a vine grower, Noah learned the fermenting process by which wine is made and became drunk from wine. No moral evil was attached by the writer to what Noah had done. However, in his drunken state he lay uncovered and his son Ham saw him lying naked. To look on the naked body of any person who was a family member or relative was considered by the ancient Hebrews to be a terribly gross evil and was prohibited (see Lev. 18:6–18).

The continuing toll of sin (9:24–25).—Ham saw his naked father and told his brothers Shem and Japheth about it. They, in turn, discreetly took a cover and backed in to put it over Noah. The following verses present problems. Noah awoke and knew what his *youngest son* had done to him (v. 24). But Japheth was the youngest son of Noah, while it was Ham who was recorded to have seen his naked father. Then Noah voiced a curse upon Canaan, the son of Ham. Could it be that "the youngest son" referred to Canaan, the grandson? It may have been that Canaan saw the naked grandfather first and told Ham, who, for curiosity, checked and saw his naked father before telling Shem and Japheth. This may explain why Canaan alone of all the grandchildren was included in this story and why the curse was placed on Canaan rather than Ham.

There is another possible reason for the curse being placed on Canaan if, in fact, he was not the one who looked on his naked grandfather. The curse may have been Noah's way of declaring that the character of Ham would so blight the lives of his children that it would be a curse upon them for generations (see Ex. 20:5). Hundreds of years later, when Genesis was completed, the Canaanites that the Hebrews knew were an immoral, profligate, and idolatrous people.

Note should be taken that the curse was not placed on Ham, the ancestor of black-skinned people. It is consequently a tragic misinterpretation of Scripture to identify black skin color as a curse, resulting from the curse of Ham's skin. What was the nature of the curse placed on Canaan? It was that he should serve his brothers (uncles) Shem and Japheth, who had proved more wise and moral than he. There is no indication that the curse was to pass to his descendants, except through the influence of his character upon them.

A blessing promised (9:26–27).—Sin was still present, creating continued disharmony between God and mankind. But integrity was also present, and it brought its inherent blessing. Noah declared that Shem would be blessed and Japheth would be enlarged. The writer again identified Yahweh as the source of Shem's blessing, just as he had identified Yahweh as the true God worshiped by Seth (4:26). Japheth would grow great because he would live in the range of Shem's influence. God did promise Abram (a grandson of Shem) that by him all the peoples of the earth would be blessed (12:3). Centuries later the descendants of Japheth formed the great center of the Christian movement as the result of the missionary preaching of Paul, a Hebrew and a descendant of Shem.

Another chapter closed (9:28).—With the recording of the death of Noah, the genealogy of Genesis 5:1–32 was closed. The era from creation to flood was covered in the stories of humanity from Adam to Noah. The record of mankind for the next period of history, from the flood to the Hebrew patriarchs, was centered around the three sons of Noah and their descendants. That record is often called the "table of the nations."

From one blood all nations (10:1–32).—In the genealogy of chapter 10, the writer of Genesis accounted for all the people and nations of the then known world. The record sets forth a broad knowledge of the history, geography, and culture of the ancient era that covered hundreds of years and saw the repopulation of the Middle East after the flood.

The descendants of Japheth (10:2–5) were the Indo-European people. They spread to settle and live in the region from the Aegean Sea to the Caspian Sea. The descendants of Ham (10:6–20) were the African and Arabic people. They spread to settle and live in Africa and the region from the Red Sea eastward as far as the Persian Gulf. The descendants of Shem (10:21–31) were the Hebrews and kindred peoples who lived in the fertile crescent, the region from Palestine through Syria, Assyria, and the Mesopotamian valley.

In the world known to the ancient Hebrews, these were all the peoples and nations of the world. They had all come from one family, the sons of Noah.

The tower of Babel (11:1–9).—Like the story of the race of giants (6:1–4), the story of Babel is a parenthesis in the record, included to explain a major happening in human history. Babel intended to explain why there are so many languages and why there is so much disunity among mankind. It also illustrates the principle of divine judgment upon human arrogance.

The events at Babel obviously do not fall into historical sequence after the population developments recorded in chapter 10. The Babel experience occurred certainly very soon after the flood, when there was "one language and few words," and the people had not dispersed across the land. By contrast, the genealogy of Noah's sons describes a time when there were developing families (clan nations) and differing languages (10:5,20,31).

The goal of the people at Babel was not evil, but their spirit was certainly not in harmony with God. They feared a breakdown in their unity, and it was within their unity that they had a sense of identity and security. To avoid fragmentation, they set out to develop a uniting center around which they could rally and preserve their identity.

Their error was in their arrogance. They believed they could accomplish their goal by their own efforts. The evil of their motive was similar to the defiant rebellion of Adam and Eve against the sovereignty of God. The people at Babel ignored God as though they had no need of him at all.

They set out to build a city around a tower. That city and tower were to be the center around which they would establish their identity, maintain their unity, and develop their security. In all probability the tower they planned to build was similar to the Babylonian ziggurats. These were large mounds, built to rise above the plains of Mesopotamia. On top of the mound, towers were built as central places of pagan worship. People who worshiped the moon and stars could climb the mounds and towers to get nearer to their gods and have unhindered views of their objects of worship.

The Babylonian name for the place called Babel was a word that meant the gate of God. It was as though the ambitious people of Babel would build a tower and make it a gate unto successful life. God is described as "coming down" to see this thing that the people were attempting to do. He had to come down to see the very highest thing that people could make.

God's judgment condemned what they were doing, for when people start out on the way of ambition, nothing will stop them except total defeat. When people start trusting in their own abilities, they will rely upon themselves until it is proven that they have no abilities. So God's judgment was that their languages should be confused to thwart their ambitious arrogance.

Factional division resulted, as it often does, when ambitious people struggle to make a thing for themselves. The nature of the confusion of their language is not described. There are many ways in which people "do not speak the same language." Sometimes people do not use the same words. Sometimes they do not mean the same things by the words they use. Whatever the nature of the confusion, there was a breakdown of communication at Babel. The result was that what was called a "gate of God" became a "place of confusion." (The name Babel is akin to a Hebrew word which means to mix up or to confuse.)

This scattering of humanity was another decisive turning point for mankind. Sin had again reached epidemic proportions in the self-reliance of mankind, who disregarded God as though he had no place in life. The first humanity perished in the flood. Now the second humanity was scattered by confusion, suspicion, and alienation. Factional division was not God's original intent for mankind. Alienation was the result of sin running its rampant course in human life.

Narrowing the focus (11:10–32).—The purpose of the writer of Genesis was to move through the broad sweep of pre-Hebrew humanity and develop a specific focus upon the line of the Hebrew covenant people. He started with a focus on God, and he maintained that focus on God's dealing with the humanity he had created. But the writer constantly narrowed the focus within humanity to show how God came to have a covenant with a chosen people through Abraham and the Hebrew nation.

The sons of Adam were introduced, and the line of Seth was followed to Noah. The sons of Noah were recorded, and the line of Shem was followed to Terah and Abraham. That is the meaning of the genealogy in the last part of chapter 11. The focus finally came upon Abram, the first of the patriarchs. Terah's death was recorded, and the ancient record of pre-Hebrew history was closed.

Abram was born while the Terah clan lived in Ur, a city in lower Mesopotamia, west of the Euphrates River. Terah took part of his family and migrated northwestward about five hundred miles to Haran. He settled there for the rest of his life. The death of Terah was recorded to close this section of genealogy. Abram was left as the central character in the ongoing story of God and humanity.

From the broad sweep of all nations of sinful humanity, the writer has narrowed the focus to one nation. That one nation would in turn become the channel for God's work of grace to reach out again to all nations, as the promise to Abraham indicated (see 12:3). The stage was set for the beginning of another new period in the marvelous history of God's steadfast love for mankind.

Part II

The Patriarchal Period of Hebrew History

Abraham, the First Patriarch of a Covenant People

12:1 to 25:18

The call of Abram fits well the beautiful proclamation of Isaiah 43:19. God said, "Behold, I am doing a new thing; now it springs forth, do you not perceive it?" Through the call of Abram, God began a new chapter in his dealing with mankind. He was establishing a covenant people to be his chosen instrument for revelation and redemption in the world. God was indeed doing a new thing.

Background of Abram's Call

Hebrew history did not begin in Canaan. It began in Mesopotamia, in a city named Ur. That city was a center of Sumerian culture and moon worship in Abram's day. The political and social situations in that area were in ferment, however, due to encroaching pressure from migrating Amorites.[1] As a result there was significant instability there, and Ur was not the most desirable place to live at that time.

No reason is given in the Bible for Terah's decision to leave Ur. He and Abram may well have chosen to migrate to another place in search of a more settled environment. They did leave Ur with the intention of going to Canaan (11:31). And Canaan was at that time within the orbit of Egyptian influence. Egypt was quite stable and in the golden age of its world influence, in contrast to the turmoil and uncertainty in Mesopotamia.[2] If Terah and Abram were interested in moving to a more settled place, Canaan would have been an appropriate choice.

The geographic relationship of Ur and Canaan brings into focus the significance of what has been called "the fertile crescent." That land area stretches like a half-moon around the northern perimeter of the Arabian desert from the Persian Gulf in the east to Egypt in the west. It included the ancient empires of Chaldea, Assyria, Syria, and Egypt. Caravans and armies moved back and forth through that crescent as the empires struggled for economic, political, and military supremacy. That was the environment in which Abram made his migration and in which the Hebrew nation began and developed through a thousand years of its history.

Terah and Abram left Ur and moved to Haran. There is no indication that Ur had any continuing influence upon their lives. Terah settled down at Haran and did not complete the planned migration to Canaan. He may have found there the settled situation he was seeking, or he may have simply been tired of moving after the long journey up most of the length of the Euphrates River. In Haran he found a city that was linked by commerce with his native Ur. Haran was also a center of moon worship as Ur had been. Terah made Haran his home for the rest of his life.

Abram, by contrast, stayed in Haran for only a period of time. He moved on to Canaan, and that move was clearly the result of a sense of divine calling. When and how God called Abram is not certain. The implication at the beginning of chapter 12 is that Abram was in Haran when he received his special call. He was called to leave Terah's clan, as he did at Haran—not migrate with them, as he had from Ur to Haran. He *may* have received some sense of divine call in Ur before they began to move. He *certainly did* receive a call from God in Haran.

There is not even a hint of how God's call came to Abram, whether by dream, or vision, or inspired insight into the meaning of conditions in the surrounding world. Whatever the means used, Abram heard. He may have left Ur with Terah because they were dissatisfied with pagan moon worship or unsettled living conditions. He left Haran and Terah's clan to go to Canaan because God called him into a new covenant relationship. Abram was to go away from the religious and family environment in which he had lived. He was to go to a new land and begin a new life with the true God.

Call to Covenant (12:1–3)

The concept of covenant was not new. God made a covenant with Noah before the flood: If he would trust God and come into the ark, then God would preserve his family through the flood (6:18). God made another covenant after the flood: He would never again destroy the earth and life upon it by a flood (9:11). In the first instance the covenant was conditional upon the people sharing in it. The second was an unconditional promise.

God's covenant with Abram had a new and distinctive dimension. He was seeking a faithful people through whom he could do a redemptive work in the world. So God called Abram to enter into covenant with him and to become the originator and ancestor of a nation of people who would live in covenant with God. Note that the word covenant does not appear in these verses that record the call of Abram. In Genesis 15:18, however, the relation between God and Abram is described as a covenant relationship, and the concept of covenant became central in the Hebrew conviction about their relationship with God. They became "the covenant people" because they were the descendants of Abram and shared in the covenant God had made with him. So God's call of Abram to a covenant relationship was especially crucial for the Hebrews. It became a focus for their development as a people and for all their subsequent national history.

Abram's requirement (12:1-3).—Two things were required of Abram. The first was an act of trusting obedience. Abram was called to make a break with the past, to leave the land and the heritage of his parental clan. He was called to go to a new land, to make a new beginning, and to become the founder of a new nation in the land to which God would lead him.

Such a venture would indeed require great faith on Abram's part. Maintaining ties with family and homeland had an importance for ancient people that modern people can rarely understand. In the ancient east it was through belonging to one's clan that a person had identity and security.[3] Such a sense of family solidarity would have bound Abram to Terah's clan. The idea of separating himself from the heritage of his family would have involved a great sense of threat to his personal identity and future. Yet that separation from his heritage was the very thing Abram was called to do. His mission was not to perpetuate the heritage of his ancestry. His mission was to begin with God a new stream of life and heritage.

The second requirement for Abram was that he become a channel for God's universally redemptive work in the world. God declared his intention and revealed his concern for the world in saying to

Abram, "In you all the families of the earth shall be blessed" (12:3).

With the requirement that Abram was to have a role of service in the covenant relationship, God made a promise that had universal dimensions. Abram's descendants were to become a covenant nation, but God's plan encompassed all the other nations of the world as well. The Hebrew nation was to have a special role but not an exclusive relationship with God. The other people of the world were God's people too, and the purpose of God's covenant with Abram was to establish a channel for bringing God's blessing to the people and leading the people to have faith in God.

Abram was called to a relationship with God in which he would both receive blessing and be an instrument of blessing. It is always tragic when a person or a people sees their relationship with God only as a source of benefit, without at the same time perceiving the dimension of stewardship that blessing involves. God's gifts bless most richly not when they are "possessed," but when they are permitted to flow through life like a stream of living water.

God's promise (12:2–3).—As his part of the covenant, God promised that Abram and his descendants would become a substantial and richly blessed nation among the peoples of the earth. Abram was promised that God would cause his name (his identity and his reputation) to become great. The very thing that the people at Babel tried arrogantly to achieve by their own efforts (11:4), God promised to give to Abram as a blessing when he lived in covenant relationship with him. Abram would be giving up his identity and security as a part of the clan heritage of his fathers when he separated from Terah and left Haran to go live in Canaan. In this promise God assured him that he would be compensated for what he gave up by what he would gain to replace it. Abram's name and renown would be far greater as the first patriarch of God's covenant people than it could have ever become merely as "son of Terah" of Ur and Haran.

Abram was assured also that he and his people would possess a national homeland. Thus they would have an established identity as a people, and as such they could be an influence to bring light and blessing to other nations of people in the world.

God's promise was made out of his sovereign capacity as God to provide help and blessing. His promise reflects his concern for the Hebrew people and for all the peoples of the world. Abram's obedient and trusting response to become a covenant person was essential for the covenant relationship offered by God to become an effective reality. What God would do for Abram and the world waited on Abram's response, but the initiative was God's. The story of redemption, like the story of creation, began with God speaking. Both creation and redemption are products of God's initiation and action. God called Abram into a covenant and began to do something redemptive for sinful humanity. How would Abram, and mankind, respond?

Seeking God's Will (12:4 to 14:24)

A Nomad in Search of a Home (12:4 to 13:18)

Abram went. In response to God's call, he left Haran to travel toward Canaan. His age was 75 when he left Haran. He died at age 175 (25:7). For the century in between he "sojourned in the land of promise, as in a foreign land, living in tents with Isaac and Jacob" (Heb. 11:9). His way of life in Canaan was the way of life of a seminomad. He had come to Canaan out of a strong sense of call, however, so this was not a mere migration. Abram was on mission.

Abram did not leave Haran empty-handed. Even while he had lived within Terah's clan for seventy-five years, Abram had been accumulating possessions of his own. So had Lot, the nephew of Abram who went with him from Haran on to Canaan. They had flocks of sheep and herds of cattle, along with servants to herd them and the tents that were a part of their wandering pastoral style of life. Abram and Sarai, along with Lot, took with them all their servants and possessions when they migrated to what was to be their new homeland.

New places in a new land (12:6–9).—The first stop Abram made in Canaan was at Shechem. Shechem was in the center in the land of Canaan, about thirty miles south of the Sea of Galilee and fifteen miles west of the Jordan River, not far from the location where Samaria was later built.

The "oak of Moreh" was there. The word *moreh* means teaching. Apparently the place was a Canaanite religious center, probably where people came to receive oracles (authoritative religious proclamations) from the pagan Canaanite gods. In that place God appeared to Abram with a promise: "To your descendants I will give this land"

(12:7). That promise had two significant meanings. First, it identified the land of Canaan as the land God had promised to the people of Abram for a national homeland. Second, it indicated that a new religious day was dawning. At a center of pagan religion God was declaring his sovereignty. He was the God of that land, and he would displace the idol gods which were being worshiped there. Abram built an altar to acknowledge the sovereignty of God at that place.

Abram moved southward another fifteen miles and came to Bethel. Leaving Bethel, Abram went on southward still another fifty miles to the Negeb, a desert region south of Beer-sheba.

Why did Abram keep moving? No indication is given in the text of any conflict between him and the inhabitants of the places where he had stopped. However he was received in those places, they apparently did not seem to him to be the place he was seeking to establish his new home.

By observing the style of life that Abram and his descendants followed until the time of the migration into Egypt, we can gain some insight into the way Abram was probably thinking as he searched for a place to settle. The patriarchs were not desert nomads, wandering at will without possessions and living by raiding and plunder. But neither were they farmers and vinedressers. They were seminomad stockherders who wandered on the fringes of the more settled tribes in the land.

Therefore, Abram was likely not warmly welcomed by the settled Canaanite tribes at Shechem or Bethel. Apparently he kept moving on, looking for an area where he could move about almost at will with his grazing herds.

When he came to the Negeb he found such a place. That area was not well suited for settled living. Down until the tenth century B.C. it was peopled largely by wandering shepherds who roamed over its arid hills in search of the sparse grazing and water for their flocks.[4] The Canaanites, who were agricultural people, did not care for the Negeb; so there would be no conflict with them if Abram grazed his herds in that region. He was moving about, touching new places in an unfamiliar new land. He was a nomad in search of a home.

To Egypt in search of food (12:10–20).—A famine developed in Canaan, for its arid conditions made that land subject to periodic droughts. Egypt, with its annual overflow of the Nile River, had the most dependable food supply in the whole region. In times of famine the people in Canaan looked to Egypt for a food supply (see 41:56 to 42:2).

Due to the famine in Canaan, Abram went to Egypt in search of food. There he did a shrewd but foolish thing. He believed that the Egyptians would be struck by Sarai's beauty and that he might be killed so that some Egyptian might have her for his harem. Abram and Sarai schemed to identify her as his sister instead of his wife. Abram was willing to endanger Sarai's honor for his safety. He did not come through as a very good example of morality or husbandly devotion in that event.

Events developed just as Abram had foreseen. The Egyptians were impressed with Sarai's beauty, and she was taken into the king's harem. He in turn heaped gifts upon Abram, both livestock and servants. The statement by the king "I took her for my wife" (v. 19) does not mean that they were living in a one-to-one husband-wife relationship as Abram and Sarai did. The situation most likely reflected an ancient harem practice. Kings and wealthy nobles gathered numerous women into their harems for prestige and for their pleasure. Many times the women in the harems were placed there by political agreements between kings and tribal chiefs as part of their alliances to be friends instead of enemies. The Egyptian king seems to have thought of this situation in that way until he learned that Sarai was Abram's wife instead of his sister. Abram feared to make the courageous move and identify his relationship to Sarai.

But God intervened. A plague, which they perceived to be divinely imposed, developed in the pharaoh's house. The king then realized that Sarai was really Abram's wife. Though he had earlier showered Abram with gifts (12:16), now he reproached Abram, returned his wife to him, and expelled them from the land. He sent a military escort with them to make sure they left Egypt. They were fortunate that the king did nothing more in retaliation than to deport them. So Abram returned to Canaan with all the possessions he had taken when he went to Egypt.

Realigning the clan (13:1-18).—When Terah left Ur, he took his orphaned grandson Lot along with him to Haran (11:27-28,31). When Abram left Haran, he took his nephew with him on to Canaan (12:4). Lot had continued to be a part of Abram's clan even though through the years he had accumulated his own flocks and herds. After they returned from Egypt to the Negeb (13:1), it became evident that the clan would have to be divided and realigned. One area with its sparse grazing could support only limited numbers of sheep and cattle. Abram and Lot had been developing even larger numbers of livestock. In the Negeb where water and grass were scarce, larger and larger grazing areas were required to take care of their needs. Even after they left the Negeb and moved to the region of Bethel, there still was not adequate grass and water for them in one place. In addition to Abram and Lot, they also had to compete with the Canaanites and Perizzites who lived in that region for the land and water resources available there (13:7).

Strife developed between the herdsmen of Abram and Lot. Abram was wise enough to know that the other inhabitants of the land would take advantage of any disunity within their ranks. Nor did he want animosity to develop between himself and his nephew. So he proposed a division, with each taking a separate grazing area for his cattle and sheep.

Abram demonstrated a very generous spirit. He suggested that Lot choose first the area he preferred, while Abram was willing to accept another area. Lot chose what seemed to be the most desirable part of the land, the southern Jordan valley with its well-watered and fertile land and the cities of Zoar, Sodom, and Gomorrah in the region then south of the Dead Sea. But that choice proved to be unwise. Dwelling in the valleys, Lot was exposed to the influence of the worshipers of pagan gods who were believed to control the fields and flocks of the lowland agricultural areas. Living in the cities of the pagan Canaanites, Lot was under the influence of the evil that later brought about the destruction of Sodom and Gomorrah.

Abram was left to go to the hill country west and south of Bethel. That rugged mountain country was believed to be the land of El Shaddai, the Almighty God, a God of rugged majesty (17:1). This God later revealed himself as Yahweh to Moses on the mountain of Sinai. From the great central mountains of Canaan, Abram was told to look in every direction as far as he could see. He was promised all that land for a homeland for himself and his numerous descendants.

He walked "through the length and breadth of the land" in his early wanderings over Canaan. In those early travels he touched many of the places later prominent in Hebrew history. In most of the places where he stopped, Abram built altars and worshiped God to express his sense of the presence and leadership of God.

Were Abram's travels the caravan movements of a merchant prince or the nomad movements of a herdsman grazing his sheep and cattle? They may have been a combination of both. He was rich in cattle, but also in silver and gold (13:2). Commercial trade routes certainly passed through many of the central points where his tents were pitched from time to time.

In the southern hill country of Canaan, Abram found his home. He chose Hebron as the place to settle, as much as a nomad herdsman or merchant prince would ever be settled. There he set up his tents and called it home. There, as in so many other places, he built an altar and worshiped God.

Establishing a Place Among Princes (14:1–24)

This account of Abram's defeat of the coalition of kings describes the purpose of his expedition as the rescue of Lot, who had been captured and kidnapped. Lot, however, plays only a minor role in the event. The focus is upon Abram and the establishment of his place of power and influence. This story is independent of both what had gone before and what would follow. The most important information revealed by the events recorded here is that Abram had come to have an established place among the princes of the land.

The military lineup (14:1–12).—A coalition of kings from Mesopotamia and eastward made a military invasion into the region around the Dead Sea. There they engaged in war with a coalition of kings from that area. There is no positive historical identification of the kings; nor is there any certain geographical identification of some of the places named in the account. Very probably these were tribal chiefs rather than kings of established nations. No reason for the invasion is given, but it has been suggested that they may have been trying to force open some caravan routes through the area.

The Mesopotamian coalition subjected the Siddim valley forces and kept them under control for a dozen years. Then the valley forces rebelled, and the Mesopotamian armies had to put down that uprising.

The eastern kings made a thorough sweep through the Siddim valley, looted their cities, and went away. They took Lot as a captive and his possessions as spoils of war (14:12). This abduction of Lot was what caused Abram to get involved.

Abram to the rescue (14:13–16).—News was brought to Abram at

Mamre (near Hebron) about what had happened to Lot. Abram gathered his forces and went to rescue his nephew. He is said to have
taken with him 318 trained men. Verse 24 seems to imply that 3
other men, probably with their groups of trained men, were also
involved in the expedition.

Who were those "trained men" Abram took with him? Were they
the private army of a merchant prince or a warrior chieftain, as has
been suggested? [5] If Abram was a merchant prince, he needed trained
warriors to protect his caravans of merchandise from plunder by rob-
ber bands. Any identification of Abram as a military man is not in
harmony with the larger picture of him reflected by the records of
his life. If he was a wealthy herdsman, as the Bible clearly indicates
he was, his herdsmen would have needed to be trained in military
defense to secure themselves and the herds against raids by marauding
bands. This latter traditional view of the nature of Abram's band of
trained men has more substantial support in the biblical record.

In a shrewd, aggressive night attack, Abram and his forces routed
the enemy in a battle near Damascus in Syria, something more than
150 miles to the north. They rescued Lot and his possessions, along
with some of the plunder taken from Sodom. Having accomplished
their purpose, they headed back toward their home country in southern Canaan.

Meeting with Melchizedek (14:17-24).—As the victorious proces-
sion was returning, they were met, apparently somewhere near Jerusalem, by the king of Sodom and by Melchizedek, a king in Jerusalem.
This is the only record of any association by Abram with Jerusalem
during his entire life. The status given to Melchizedek in this incident,
however, indicates the importance that Jerusalem had as a religious
center even at this early time. But Jerusalem came to have great
significance in Hebrew history only after David chose to make that
former Jebusite fortress his capital (2 Sam. 5:6-10).

Upon their meeting Melchizedek spoke a blessing upon Abram,
and Abram made a gift to him of a tenth of the spoils of battle he
had brought back. Melchizedek is identified as a "priest of the Most
High God" (14:18). There are ancient sources, outside the Bible, that
provide evidence of a cult in the Jerusalem area who worshiped "the
Highest God." [6] This was not the fully developed worship of Yahweh
as the supreme God but was more an indefinite worship of the "chief"
god—in a sense similar to the Athenians of Paul's day worshiping

"an unknown god" (Acts 17:23). It is closely akin, however, to God's revelation of himself to Abram as El Shaddai (Gen. 17:1). As with Seth (4:26) and Shem (9:26), the writer of Genesis identified the Most High God whom Melchizedek worshiped as Yahweh, who later revealed himself to Abraham and Moses as the only true God and was therefore truly as "the Most High God."

Abram returned to the king of Sodom the people he had rescued and the spoils he had recovered. The king of Sodom asked only the release of his people. He suggested that Abram keep the "goods" for himself, but Abram declined. He insisted that he would not make himself wealthy out of what belonged to another. He did consent to take the expenses of the expedition ("what the young men have eaten," v. 24), and he suggested that a share of the recovered goods be given to the other men who had helped recover them. Lot was rescued and returned to his home in Sodom, only to need rescue from the evil of that city in the future (see 19:5–28).

Conflict: Divine and Human Solutions (15:1 to 18:15)

Assurance for a Troubled Man (15:1–21)

Abram was a troubled man. He was fearful about the future because he had no son. He had left the heritage of his past when he left his native land and his father's clan. Now he had no assurance of the future, for he had no son to carry on his life beyond him. The nearest thing he had to an heir was a slave born in his house (15:3). His growing despair hung heavily upon his life. He needed assurance, and God would give it.

A renewed promise of progeny (15:1–6).—God spoke to Abram and gave him a promise of personal security and reward, but that was not enough to relieve the despair he was feeling. The best he could hope for was to live out his life and leave his heritage to an heir who was not his son. God renewed his promise that it would not be so. He had promised Abram that he would have a progeny of descendants (12:2). He made that promise even more specific. Abram's descendants would be as numerous as the stars of the heavens (15:5). His heir would be his own son, not an adopted one.

In spite of his despair, Abram was able to believe and trust that promise from God. The writer penned an editorial declaration that has stood as a benchmark of faith through the ages: "Abraham believed God, and it was reckoned to him as righteousness" (see Rom. 4:3). Abram put his trust in God and in God's promise. Through that trust he became the recipient of the fruit of his faith. To the generations who followed he became a hero of faith (Heb. 11:12). Through faith Abram received the status of righteousness before God. Righteousness, as it is used here, does not imply perfect moral behavior, for Abram had surely not reached that goal. Righteousness meant proper conduct in relationship. Since Abram had faith in the one who had made a covenant promise to him, he could trust the fulfillment of that promise and could conduct the affairs of his life accordingly.[7]

A renewed promise of a homeland (15:7–8).—God also promised again that the Hebrews, and they would be many, would have a homeland. They were promised not just any homeland, but Canaan. The word of assurance was "I . . . brought you from Ur . . . to give you *this* land" (15:7). Though Abram was already living in the land, that promise still seemed to him too good to be true, too much to even hope for. He pleaded for assurance: "How am I to know that I shall possess it?" (15:8). He needed something tangible to hold on to. Again, God would give it.

A covenant ritual (15:9–21).—Abram was instructed to prepare for a ritual ceremony to confirm God's covenant with him. The sacrificial animals were to be divided and laid apart so that the covenant makers could pass between the divided parts. To pass between such covenant sacrifices meant that the covenant parties sealed their covenant with unbreakable commitments. Abram prepared the sacrifice and waited.

As the day neared its end God caused Abram to fall into a deep sleep. Such a divinely induced trance was one of the ancient channels of dream revelations. While in his deep sleep, Abram received a revelation that was twofold in nature. It gave personal assurance but also indicated that some severe trials were yet to come. He was given advance warning of the Egyptian bondage that would come in later generations to his descendants. But God assured him of his overarching purpose. Abram would die in peace, and his children would have their homeland. He was encouraged not to lose heart because of the trials and hindrances that would be met before the goal was reached.

With those great promises made to the weary Abram, God then

put the seal of his commitment upon the covenant. In the darkness at the end of the day Abram saw, apparently in a vision, "a smoking fire pot and a flaming torch" (v. 17) pass between the divided parts of the covenant sacrifice. God affirmed his covenant with Abram. Unity would come again across the face of the earth. From Egypt to the Euphrates, the land of many peoples would become again the land of one people, the people of God. The tragic, fragmenting effects of Babel would be overcome at last. The unifying presence of the covenant people of God would finally make the world one again. God had a purpose for Abram and his descendants greater than their most expanded imaginations could conceive. God's thoughts are indeed higher than our thoughts (Isa. 55:9). He is always ahead of mankind in his wise and gracious purpose.

Inadequate Answers for Human Frustration (16:1–16)

The childless condition of Abram and Sarai has been a prominent feature in the story about them thus far. It was mentioned when they were first introduced (11:30). It was described as one of Abram's greatest concerns (15:2–3). God had responded to Abram's concern with promises about descendants he was sure to have (12:2,7; 15:4–5), but Abram's faith faltered in the face of his continued childlessness (16:1).

An attempted solution (16:2–4).—The Hebrews thought childlessness to be a tragic condition. To them, hope for the future lay in one's children through succeeding generations. To be unable to have children created a deep and disturbing frustration. Out of such frustration Abram and Sarai attempted the solution recorded in this passage.

The procedure described was legal in the society of Abram's day. It was considered quite morally acceptable. Since Sarai could not have children herself, she could use a slave maiden to bear children for her by her husband. Such a child would have been considered to belong to Sarai, not to the servant mother. So Sarai suggested that Abram have a child by Hagar, her Egyptian servant.[8] Abram agreed to that human attempt to solve their problem of childlessness. His frustration and lapse of faith combined to persuade him to try a solution that proved to be sadly inadequate and troublesome.

Hagar's reaction (16:4–6).—When Hagar realized that she was to become the mother of a child by Abram, she became haughty and contemptuous toward Sarai. After all, Hagar the slave was giving to Abram something that Sarai the wife could not. Would the servant then stand higher in the eyes of the master than his wife? Would Hagar displace Sarai as the most important woman in Abram's household? Trouble arose between Sarai and Hagar.

The trouble in the household quickly spread to involve husband and wife as well as slave and mistress. Sarai blamed Abram for letting Hagar get out of hand. Abram blamed Sarai for not being able to control her personal servant. Their trifling with the principle of monogamous fidelity in marriage had created a distressed situation for all three people involved.

Sarai chose to salve her battered ego by striking out vindictively against Hagar. She treated Hagar so heartlessly that Hagar ran away. Intolerable misery drove her to try to escape.

Predictions about Ishmael (16:7–12).—Hagar's flight took her southward from Hebron toward Kadesh (16:14). Since she was an Egyptian, it appears that she was trying to make her way to her native land. Such a trip of more than two hundred miles through the severe conditions of that desert country proved to be too much for a pregnant young woman like Hagar traveling alone. She made it for nearly half the distance. Then as she stopped by a spring to rest, the events of this passage took place.

A question came to her: "Where have you come from and where are you going?" (v. 8). Her reply that she was fleeing from Sarai brought the instruction to return and accept her servant place in Abram's household. The focus of the passage then turned to her unborn child and predictions about him. Hagar's descendants through that child would be many.

A name was given for her child. He was to be called Ishmael, a name that means "God hears." Hagar was thus assured that God was not unaware of her plight or unconcerned about what was happening to her and her child. A fearful prediction was given of the kind of person her son would turn out to be. Conflict and strife would be his way of life, "his hand against every man and every man's hand against him" (16:12). That prediction came true through generations of struggle between Ishmaelites and Israelites.

Questions arise in our minds. Did the way Ishmael and Hagar were treated by Sarai and Abram cause him to turn out to be "a wild ass of a man"? (v. 12). Was violence his way of responding to his childhood experiences of being rejected and despised? Certainly he grew up knowing that he was the first son of Abram; yet he was cast out so that he could not share the heritage of his father with Isaac, his younger half-brother. When people play loosely with morality in family relations, and when they play selfish games with the feelings of others, many hurts result. And they last for a long, long time.

Beauty in the midst of suffering (16:13–16).—Hagar received a beautiful insight out of her tragic experience. It was surely inspired. Her response to all she had experienced was that God is "a God of seeing" (v. 13). God really had seen what was going on. He had heard her cries of anguish as she fled from the harsh intolerance of Sarai. And if God could see her and hear the cries of even an outcast foreign slave fleeing through the wilderness, then surely he could see and know everything.

She was also aware that she had had a personal encounter with God and that it had not destroyed her. She questioned, "Have I really seen God and remained alive after seeing him?" (16:13). Out of her experience had come evidence that God has goodwill toward people rather than ill will. When he touches life he does good rather than evil. That revelation was crucial for Hagar, for there in the wilderness her very survival was at stake. That beautiful truth is equally crucial for every generation of people.

A name was given to the place where Hagar had met God and found him to be a source of hope. The place name preserved for later generations the meaning of Hagar's experience there. The name Beer-lahai-roi means "the well of the One who sees."

Hagar returned to Abram's house and there gave birth to Ishmael. His birth occurred fourteen years before Isaac was born to Abram and Sarai (compare Abram's ages, 16:15 and 21:5). So ended the first chapter in Abram and Sarai's inadequate attempt to solve the frustration of their childlessness. But it was only the first chapter, for a son had been born to Abram. Ishmael was not the son of promise, to be sure; but he was Abram's son. Troubles would continue in the family because of the jealousy and struggle for position that arose. Other chapters of distress and sadness would follow.

Reinforcement for a Promise (17:1 to 18:15)

The birth of Ishmael had not really solved anything for Abram and Sarai. The problem of their childlessness was as real as ever, and now the household was rife with ill will. That condition continued for thirteen years until the next recorded event took place. Doubtless Abram was in great need of the reinforcement that came from another renewal of covenant promises.

Abram's change of name (17:1–6).—God declared his sovereignty by the name he used for himself. The designation El Shaddai emphasized the supremacy of God. God's revelation of himself as God Almighty served to strengthen the trustworthiness of his promises. It also served to strengthen the significance of the new name given to Abram. The name Abram means exalted father, but that name could only deepen his frustration as long as he had no son who could be his true heir. He was given a new name, Abraham, which means father of a multitude. If his God was almighty and would make the promise of that new name come to fulfillment, then all his other promises could be trusted too.

So God renewed his covenant promise to make Abraham a great nation and to give him and his descendants a homeland. To reinforce that promise God gave him a new name to be a constant reminder of the promise. Every time the name Abraham was spoken, it would refresh his awareness that God had promised to make him the father of many descendants.

Continuing covenant promised (17:7–9).—God added a new dimension to the covenant. It was a promise that the covenant would be established with Abraham's descendants. The covenant would be an eternal covenant. In previous references of call and covenant (12:1–3; 15:18), the covenant was between God and Abraham. God had promised Abraham that he would have descendants and that they would have a homeland.

God added a new promise, the promise of a continuing covenant. He promised Abraham that he would deal with his descendants through a covenant relationship, just as he had dealt with Abraham. God would make promises to them, to one generation after another; and he would keep those promises.

But the nature of covenant would not be violated. Abraham and his descendants would have to be faithful in keeping the covenant. Otherwise the covenant could not exist and continue. If they broke the covenant by unfaithfulness, they could no longer expect to receive the promises of the covenant.

A seal of covenant given (17:10–14).—The first mention of circumcision in the Bible occurs here. This passage identifies circumcision as a sign of the covenant between God and Abraham, as a seal that both parties had bound themselves in the covenant between them. Each made a commitment to fulfill the promises of the covenant.

There is no indication that this event was seen as the origin of the practice of circumcision. The practice had been followed widely in primitive cultures and religions before that time. The Hebrews did change both the meaning and the practice of circumcision, however. The rite was usually performed by other primitive peoples at the time of puberty as a ceremony of initiation into the full status of manhood.[9]

The Hebrew practice of circumcision was performed in infancy. They circumcised at older ages only when the operation had not been done at birth. The significance of circumcision among the Hebrews was as a covenant sign. A male Hebrew child was circumcised to affirm that he was one of God's covenant people, a status involving both heritage and obligation. Each Hebrew was an heir to the promises of the covenant. Likewise, the circumcised Hebrew was under obligation to be faithful to the covenant and serve God in exclusive loyalty. So the covenant people were obligated to be circumcised, and they were obligated to keep the covenant into which they had entered with God.

Just as Abraham's new name would be a daily assurance of God's promises, the physical sign of circumcision would be a tangible reminder that God had bound himself in a covenant to give Abraham enough descendants to make him a great nation. God would not go back on his promises. He was seeking to give Abraham the support he needed to help him hold on to his part of the covenant.

Sarai's change of name (17:15–21).—God's covenant with Abraham included his wife Sarai. The promise of descendants meant *their* descendants. So Sarai was also given a new name, Sarah. No reason is given for her name change; nor is there any significant difference in the meaning of the two names. They are both variations of the root word, which means princess. A new name for both of them was evidently intended to convey the meaning that a new day and a new situation were about to come for them.

With her name change, there came a renewal of promise to Sarah that she was to have a son. That was a promise beyond the realm of credibility. Abraham simply could not believe it.

A critical point had arrived in Abraham's life. He had almost come to total despair. He had tried to secure an heir through a son born by Hagar. That attempt had failed, for Ishmael was not a mainline descendant of the covenant people whom God would use for his redemptive work in the world. In the meantime, Abraham and Sarah had grown older and they still had no son. The birth of a child to them was beyond the realm of human hope. On the verge of despair, Abraham questioned, "Why can't God accept Ishmael? Why can't Ishmael fill the role and be my heir?" He yearned for Ishmael to accept God and for God to accept Ishmael. He cried out, "O that Ishmael might live in thy sight!" (v. 18).

The answer kept turning again and again to Abraham and Sarah. The word of the Lord was "Sarah your wife shall bear you a son" (v. 19). Ishmael would become the father of a nation of people, but Isaac would be the son through whom the covenant and the work of redemption would be carried forward. And they were at last within a year of the time when his birth would take place.

Affirmation of the covenant (17:22 to 18:15).—God helped Abraham through another crisis in faith. By new names for himself and Sarah, by the covenant seal of circumcision, and by assurance that Sarah would yet have a son, Abraham received enough reinforcement that he could go on holding to the hope of his covenant with God. To reaffirm his commitment to the covenant, he had himself and all the males in his household circumcised.

The covenant was also reaffirmed by God through the three visitors, the divine messengers who stopped by Abraham's tent on their way to Sodom. Abraham greeted them and extended warm hospitality to them. The practice of hospitality, such as Abraham showed here, was an important feature of life in that ancient desert culture. In such sparsely settled areas travelers were often dependent upon Bedouin herdsmen such as Abraham for any shelter or provisions. Even a wayfarer was usually certain to receive welcome and the best food available when he came to a desert dweller's tent. It was considered a shameful thing for such hospitality to be withheld from a traveler (see Judg. 19:20). This generous hospitality was shown by Abraham without any hint that he recognized the guests as anything more than traveling tradesmen.

After appropriate preparations were made, Abraham had the men sit down to eat while he stood as host to wait on their needs. In their conversation they inquired about Sarah and spoke of God's promise that Sarah would have a son the next year. Sarah was listening from within the tent, and she laughed to herself at the apparently absurd idea that a woman of her age could have a child.

Out of the conversation exchange that followed a beautiful truth emerged. The visitor asked, "Is anything too hard [wonderful] for the Lord?" (18:14). Is anything so difficult that God cannot do it? Is anything so far above human levels that it is beyond the realm of possibility for God to do it? The implied answer is no. The overwhelming significance of the truth here revealed was that Sarah would indeed have a child. We ought never to forget that God's ways are higher than our ways (Isa. 55:9). He often causes extraordinary things to happen in very unusual ways.

The Lot Interlude (18:16 to 19:38)

The visitors who came to Abraham's tent were on a dual mission. They came as messengers to reaffirm God's promises to Abraham and Sarah. Then they were to go to investigate the great outcry against evil in Sodom and Gomorrah. They shared their second mission with Abraham; then the visitors went on their way. Abraham was left to talk with the Lord about what would happen in Sodom where Lot was living.

The dilemma of righteousness and justice (18:22–33).—In Abraham's dialogue with God, he wrestled with the problem of what happens to good when judgment falls upon evil. How much righteousness is necessary to prevent evil from bringing destruction upon itself? How many righteous people would it take to persuade God not to destroy Sodom? Fifty . . . forty . . . thirty . . . twenty . . . ten? Is God righteous if he lets an evil city go on in its evil? Is God just if he destroys the few righteous with the many evil? Not enough righteous people were found to spare the cities, so Sodom and Gomorrah were destroyed; but Lot and his two unmarried daughters were rescued. So God went on his way to do what was right, and Abraham returned to his tent convinced that God would do what was just.

The evil of Sodom (19:1–11).—When the two messengers reached Sodom, Lot greeted them and offered them the hospitality of his home. (Note that the number was reduced from three to two, giving the indication that the third was the Lord who had stayed behind to talk with Abraham.) The gross evil of the people of Sodom was reflected in their demand that Lot give up his guests for the perverted sexual satisfaction of the men of Sodom. Their repulsive desires reflected the tragic degree of degeneracy that had developed there. Lot pleaded with them to refrain from such evil. He seems to have been more concerned about a possible violation of hospitality than about the immorality of their perversion of sex. The laws of hospitality required the protection of guests as well as the provision of shelter and food. Lot offered to let them abuse his two virgin daughters if only they would not violate the sanctity of his house for the guests.

The men of Sodom would not listen to Lot. They even accused him of being an outsider. They scorned him for daring to judge them in their own city. They were ready to attack Lot himself when he was rescued by the guests and the people outside were struck with blindness.

The rescue of Lot (19:12–23).—Lot was instructed to leave Sodom with all his family because the destruction of the city was imminent. The two men who were to have married Lot's daughters scoffed at the warning. At the urgent insistence of the messengers, Lot and his family fled from Sodom to Zoar just ahead of the holocaust that destroyed the cities. Lot's wife looked back, "and she became a pillar of salt" (v. 26). Her longing love for the city with its evil was enough to destroy her. Her heart was still in Sodom, and a person can't really get away from where the heart is (see Prov. 4:23).

The destruction of Sodom (19:24–29).—The nature of the disaster that destroyed Sodom and Gomorrah is not clearly described. It is called a "rain" of "brimstone and fire" (v. 24). Did God use a volcanic eruption, an earthquake, or a combination of the two in that destructive judgment on the evil cities? There is no evidence of volcanic activity in the Dead Sea area, but there are deposits of sulphur and asphalt there. The likelihood then seems to be that an earthquake with resulting fires from sulphurous gases and asphalt were the elements that created the holocaust and caused the utter destruction and total disappearance of the two cities.

The sites of the destroyed cities have not been discovered. The location as described in the biblical test was in the Dead Sea valley area. It is quite probable that the earthquake and catastrophe that destroyed the cities created such a shift in the earth's crust that it enlarged the Dead Sea, which may now cover the places where they were.

Lot and his daughters (19:30–38).—After their narrow escape from Sodom, Lot and his daughters went to live in an isolated mountain cave. They were overwhelmed with fear because of the traumatic experience they had passed through. It appears that they thought the destruction was universal, thinking "there is not a man on earth" (v. 31) by which they might have children except their father.

The two daughters schemed to have children by their father. That incestuous relationship was born out of their desperation and fear. Each of them had a child, and their offspring became the first of the Moabites and Ammonites. This account was not written to make a moral judgment, neither condemnation nor justification, of what the daughters of Lot did. It is rather a narrative account of how they responded to the frightening events of the destruction of Sodom and a historical record of the origins of two neighboring tribes of non-Hebrew people.

Problems Along the Way (20:1–18)

In their continued movements about the land, Abraham and his family were constantly in touch with other tribal groups. Mutual fears and differing customs often caused problems between them. In Gerar, a tribal king named Abimelech took Sarah into his harem when she was identified as Abraham's sister instead of his wife. That incident was quite similar to the one recorded in chapter 12 which occurred in Egypt, but note some differences in details between the two accounts.

No reference is made in the Gerar story to Sarah's beauty. She was nearly twenty-five years older than at the time of their sojourn in Egypt, so physical attraction may not have been as important to Abimelech as it had been to the pharaoh. The Gerar story probably reflects a prevalent practice of using harem life as a way to tie clans together for political reasons.

Abimelech was warned in a dream that Sarah was Abraham's wife, while the Egyptian pharaoh had been made aware of that relationship through a plague. Genuine concern was recorded in the Gerar account

for the protected chastity of Sarah. A clear point is made twice that
Abimelech had not touched her (20:4,6). That concern reflects the
growing development of a high moral standard among the Hebrews.
Sexual immorality certainly continued, but at least it was increasingly
recognized as immoral.

Abraham was identified as a prophet who could pray for Abimelech
that the blight of barrenness might be removed from the Gerarites.
Abimelech reciprocated by giving gifts to Abraham as restitution for
his offense against him. This was in contrast to the gifts the pharaoh
had given as a dowry for Sarah. Abraham was given respected status
in Gerar, in contrast to being forcefully expelled from Egypt.

Were these two similar events, one in Egypt and one in Gerar;
or are the two events merely variations of one event that developed
through long generations of oral transmission? A later account (26:6–
11) tells of another very similar incident between a king named
Abimelech and Rebekah, the wife of Isaac. That account is also set
in Gerar. It is not the purpose of this commentary to attempt to
resolve textual questions of this type. Since three accounts appear
in the Genesis text, we will simply take note of their relationship
and seek for any insights we can discover in them.

Ecstasy and Jealousy (21:1–21)

The long-awaited birth of a son to Abraham and Sarah finally came
to pass. Into that one event there was focused the realization of a
dream, the fulfillment of a promise, and the continuation of a covenant
of purpose. Abraham's longing for a son had seemed like a dream,
but at last that dream had come true. God had made a promise that
Abraham would have many descendants and be a great nation, and
at last that promise had begun to be fulfilled. The covenant God
had made with Abraham would be continued to this son of promise,
and through him to the nation God would use in his redemptive
work in the world.

But the picture was not all bright. Ishmael and Hagar were still
on the scene in Abraham's house. The domestic friction that had already caused trouble would create more sorrow. The birth of a son
to Abraham and Sarah proved to be an event blessed by ecstasy but
blighted by jealousy.

The birth of Isaac (21:1-7).—There was no question in Abraham's mind that this son of promise was a divine gift. He and Sarah had been unable to have children through their years of natural reproductive ages. Now when they were very old, he a hundred and she ninety, they were going to have a son. The certainty that Isaac's birth was extraordinary became a part of the Hebrew heritage. They believed that God had miraculously caused the birth of their ancestor to guarantee the existence of the Hebrew nation as a chosen people. The account of Isaac's birth in the Genesis record expresses that faith very clearly. It was because "the Lord visited" (v. 1) Sarah that she conceived and Isaac was born to her and Abraham.

Abraham circumcised his newborn son to confirm that he was born within the covenant of God and was one of God's covenant people. He named his son Isaac, a name that means laughter, as an expression of his great joy at the birth of his son. Sarah also affirmed that joy by declaring that others would rejoice with her in the long-awaited blessing that had come to her. While there is no hint of it in the text, one might also wonder if Sarah felt some vindictive glee at getting even with Hagar for her earlier contempt (16:4). The adage "He who laughs last laughs best" may well have described how Sarah felt toward Hagar as she anticipated the birth of her son.

The birth of Isaac was an event of great joy for Abraham and Sarah. For so long they had waited and dreamed. For a long time they would have been past having any hope except for the promise of God. They had every reason to be grateful and ecstatic with joy. But the event was not without its sad side. There lurked in the background the ill will between Sarah and Hagar. Sarah's jealousy marred the joy of the blessing of Isaac's birth.

Jealousy breeds strife (21:8-11).—Though Sarah had been the originator of the plan for Abraham to have a child by Hagar (16:2-4), she had resented both Hagar and Ishmael with an animosity that bordered on hatred. After her son Isaac was born, she saw Ishmael as a threat to Isaac's position in the family. After all, Ishmael was the older son by fourteen years. Sarah did not want Ishmael to stay in the household and inherit even the smallest part of the heritage of his father.

It has been supposed that Sarah's insistence that Ishmael be banished was due to some misbehavior by Ishmael. Sarah's deep-seated jealousy and resentment appear to be the cause of the domestic strife described in this passage. Not only was she unwilling to accept Ishmael as a half-brother of Isaac; she was not even willing to tolerate his presence in the family. Sarah insisted that Hagar and Ishmael be expelled from the household.

That domestic strife brought sadness to Abraham. After all, Ishmael was his son—by an Egyptian maid who was not his wife, it was true. Nevertheless, Abraham loved him. He was hurt at the idea of sending his son away, and at first he did not seem willing to let Sarah have her way.

Dividing the line (21:12-21).—Only Isaac's covenant role finally persuaded Abraham to send Ishmael away. The development of the Hebrew nation would be through Isaac and his descendants. Therefore, Ishmael would be let go; but at his going Abraham was promised that Ishmael too would become a nation because he was Abraham's son.

Abraham sent Hagar away with Ishmael. Taking the provisions he gave them, they went to dwell in the wilderness of Beer-sheba, south from Hebron toward the Negeb and Egypt. Ishmael is called a child, and the implication is that he was totally dependent on Hagar. This part of the account is difficult to reconcile with the fact that he was probably about seventeen years old at the time of this incident. He was fourteen when Isaac was born, and Isaac had been weaned before Ishmael was banished. There seems to be no apparent answer to this problem of interpretation.

As the severe desert began to take its toll, and as their provisions began to dwindle, Ishmael's life was endangered by fatigue and thirst. But God had not forsaken them. He led Hagar to a well of water that supplied one of their vital needs. A message was given to Hagar that God had heard the cries of Ishmael, just as he had heard her cries when earlier she had wandered as an outcast in the wilderness (16:11).

Ishmael and Hagar were sustained by God's providing care. Ishmael grew to manhood and made his home in the wilderness of Paran, a hundred miles farther to the south. Under the influence of his mother, he married an Egyptian. There the nation of Ishmaelites began to develop.

The lines of Ishmael and Isaac were thus divided. No further mention was made of Ishmael until he joined Isaac to bury their father at the time of his death (25:9). The focus on Genesis was kept upon Isaac because he was the son of Abraham through whom the covenant people of God developed.

Careful Diplomacy (21:22–34)

Abraham and Abimelech kept crossing paths in their grazing movements, as they had earlier at Gerar (20:1–18). In order to avoid conflict, Abimelech approached Abraham and proposed a pact of mutual trust and nonaggression. Abraham agreed, and they made a convenant. That did not keep their herdsmen from running afoul of one another, however.

Abimelech's herdsmen seized a well that Abraham had dug, and Abraham brought the matter up with Abimelech. Abimelech insisted that he knew nothing about it, and they resolved the matter peacefully. Abraham then gave Abimelech seven lambs to seal their agreement that the well really did belong to Abraham. This was an example of wise diplomacy on the part of both men. They were making a genuine effort to live in peace, even though they often grazed their herds over the same areas.

An event of this type reflects the importance of a water source in the arid area of southern Canaan. It reveals also the need for a relationship of trust between people who touch lives as they go about their daily work.

The name of the well was Beer-sheba, "well of an oath." That name would be a constant reminder to both parties of the covenant they had made there concerning the ownership of the well.

Abimelech moved away toward the west into the land of the Philistines, along the southeastern Mediterranean coast. For some time following this, Abraham lived on good terms with the Philistines. Apparently he grazed his herds through their area without conflict. While he had made some bad blunders, as in Egypt and at Gerar (12:10–20; 20:1–18), Abraham also demonstrated wise statesmanship, as with the king of Sodom and with Abimelech at Beer-sheba (14:21–24; 21:22–34).

Ready to Give the Best (22:1–19)

Abraham's faith, which had already gone through so many times of testing, met its supreme test in the sacrifice of Isaac. Human sacrifice was a well-known practice by the Canaanites among whom Abraham lived, but there is no record of it among his ancestors.

Giving his best (22:1-14).—To sacrifice Isaac would be to sacrifice all that he had. He had given up his past when he left the land and the household of his father. He had sent away his other son, Ishmael. Isaac was all he had. To sacrifice him would be to give up his present and his future. No more complete test of devotion to God could have been laid upon Abraham than this call to sacrifice his beloved son as a burnt offering.

We can only surmise how heavy his heart was as Abraham traveled three days with Isaac toward a place and a time of destiny. He went to Mount Moriah with the full intention of sacrificing his son as a burnt offering to God. In his heart he had already made the complete commitment of his son, the best thing he had in all the world, to his God. His utter devotion to God could not have been greater if he had actually burned Isaac on the altar that day.

The climax of the event occurred, however, when Abraham laid his son bound on the altar and God would not let him do the final killing and burning. Abraham was blessed for his unlimited devotion. God said, "Do not lay your hand on the lad . . . for I know you fear God, seeing you have not withheld your son" (22:12).

A lasting influence (22:15-19).—Abraham's readiness to give his best, without exception, made a lasting mark on Hebrew life. His example of utter devotion influenced multitudes of his descendants for centuries to follow. A by-product of the event was a prohibition of human sacrifice among the Hebrews. It was henceforth considered a gross offense against God to make a human sacrifice (see 2 Kings 16:3).

This first patriarch of the Hebrew people experienced a great victory in that test of his faith. He learned a significant lesson from God through the event. Out of Abraham's experience God was able to carry forward his revelation through the prophets to the generations that would follow. Twelve hundred years later Isaiah would cry out in the name of God, "I have had enough of burnt offerings, . . cease to do evil, learn to do good; seek justice, correct oppression" (Isa. 1:11,16-17). Micah would ask, "Shall I give my first-born for my transgression?" And he would answer, "What does the Lord require of you but to do justice, and to love kindness, and to walk humbly with your God" (Mic. 6:7-8). And in the New Testament, Paul's great appeal was "to present your bodies as a *living* sacrifice, holy and acceptable to God" (Rom. 12:1). When Abraham made the commitment of his very best to God, all who would come after him were given beautiful revelations of the sacrifice of devotion that God wants from those who would serve him.

Striking a Tent (22:20 to 25:18)

After the birth of Isaac, the story of Abraham was quickly closed. Only a few incidents about Abraham are recorded from that following seventy-five-year period. The events recorded are significant, however.

Rebekah was introduced (22:20–24).—The genealogy of Nahor is important because he was the grandfather of Rebekah. The last reference to him had been as a son of Terah and a brother of Abraham in Ur (11:27,29). He had apparently followed his father from Ur to Haran, for Haran had become his clan home by the time Isaac was a young man.

National origin was very important to the ancient Hebrews, so they were always concerned about the heritage of a person being married. The lineage of Nahor clearly established Rebekah as a cousin of Isaac.

The death of Sarah (23:1–20).—When Isaac was thirty-seven years old, Sarah died (17:17; 23:1). That was thirty-eight years before the death of Abraham, but in a very real way it was the beginning of the end of his life. Sarah died at Hebron, the most established home they had had in Canaan. Abraham was deeply grieved at her death because a great love had existed between them.

Securing a burial place was something Abraham could not avoid after Sarah's death. Abraham went to the Hittites and asked if he might buy some place for a burial ground. The story of the bargaining reveals a typical Oriental pattern. The Hittites suggested that Abraham just use any of their established burial sites. But that would have left him with no established property rights. Abraham, in turn, identified the place he wanted and insisted that he would pay full price for it. The bargaining was then between Abraham and the owner of that particular plot of ground rather than with the larger Hittite group. Ephron, the owner of the land, suggested that he would give the piece of ground to Abraham. But Abraham wanted to maintain a freedom from indebtedness to the Hittites, so he insisted on paying for the property. Ephron quoted a price, believed by many to have been far above the actual value of the land. Abraham paid the price and bought the land in a public transaction. At last he owned a piece of the promised land.

Abraham buried Sarah in the cave of Machpelah and established a family burial ground. Later others were buried there, including Abraham himself (25:9), Isaac (35:29), Rebekah and Leah (49:31), and Jacob (50:13).

A wife for Isaac (24:1–67).—After the death of Sarah, Abraham became more keenly aware of his advancing years. A task of major importance to him was to secure a wife for Isaac. In the culture of that time the arranging of marriages was a parental prerogative; but it was not an exclusive practice, as can be noted later in the case of Esau and Jacob.

Abraham sent a servant to Haran, to the clan home of his father and brother. He charged the servant not to choose a Canaanite woman for Isaac to marry or to take Isaac from Canaan to any other land to marry. Rebekah, a second cousin of Isaac, lived at Haran with her family and was chosen to be the wife for Isaac. See the following chapter for a more detailed discussion of this event as a part of the life of Isaac.

Another wife for Abraham (25:1–6).—Abraham married Keturah, and they had six children. Their names indicate that they became ancestors of Arabic tribes who lived on the desert borderlands east of Canaan. It is indicated in the passage that Keturah was more like a concubine than a true wife. Her children were treated more like outcast stepchildren (as Ishmael had been) than like genuine children. They were sent away from Abraham's house, while Isaac was given all the family heritage. Serious animosities developed between the Hebrews and their cast-off kindred because of such moral failures within their parental families. These Hebrew-Arabic hostilities have continued even down to modern times.

The death of Abraham (25:7–10).—Abraham died at age 175, as one of the most significant persons of all human history. He was the progenitor of a family line that has continued to exist as an identifiable people unto the present.

His sons Isaac and Ishmael buried him with Sarah in the cave at Machpelah. Their common sorrow brought them together; and for a little while at least, they laid aside their resentments and hostility in order to share the grief and loss of their father's death.

Summary (25:11–26).—Death removed Abraham from the scene.
Isaac and his sons were brought into focus as the channel through
which God's covenant was carried forward. Isaac is described as having
established his place of residence at Beer-lahai-roi, an oasis south of
the Negeb where Hagar had stopped in her flight from Sarah (16:14).
He was ready to take his place as the clan leader of his father's house
after Abraham's death.

First, however, before developing that record, the writer of Genesis
set down a genealogy of Ishmael to close the story of his place in
Abraham's lineage. Verse 18 seems to indicate that Ishmael was hastily
alienated from all his kindred.

The account of the birth of Isaac's sons effectively concludes the
story of Abraham and completes the transition from Abraham, the
first patriarch, to his son. And the story would go on, for God had a
purpose to work out through his covenant people. The tent of Abraham had been struck and folded. Another tent, that of Isaac, stood
bold against the sky. A new patriarch followed the fallen giant. God
was not finished. His work would go on.

Notes

1. John Bright, *A History of Israel* (Philadelphia: The Westminster Press,
1972), pp. 48–49.

2. G. Ernest Wright and Floyd V. Filson, *The Westminster Historical Atlas
to the Bible* (Philadelphia: The Westminster Press, 1945), p. 25a.

3. Walter Eichrodt, *Theology of the Old Testament* 2 (Philadelphia: The
Westminster Press, 1967), p. 233.

4. Bright, p. 80.

5. Gerhard von Rad, *Genesis* (Philadelphia: The Westminster Press, 1971),
p. 175.

6. Ibid., p. 179.

7. Ibid., p. 185.

8. Bright, p. 78.

9. Cuthbert A. Simpson, *The Interpreter's Bible* 1 (New York: Abingdon
Press, 1952), p. 613.

Isaac: The Overshadowed Giant
21:1 to 35:29

When Isaac was born he fulfilled a long-delayed promise of God to Abraham and Sarah. He was also the answer to a long-frustrated hope and dream of theirs (21:1-7). His birth was not an unmixed blessing, however. Sarah's harsh jealousy toward Ishmael and Hagar created problems. Against his will Abraham was urged by Sarah to disown Ishmael and banish him and Hagar from the household. Abraham consented only when he was convinced that Isaac was to be the bearer of the covenant heritage.

So Isaac was born as a son of promise. He was reared with the clear indication of unique vocation surrounding him. He was to fulfill the promise of God that a nation of people with special purpose would arise from the descendants of Abraham. Isaac has an established place as the second of the Hebrew patriarchs, but there is really very little about him recorded in the Bible. The early part of his life was lived under the shadow of his illustrious father, Abraham, while the latter part of his life was lived under the shadow of his aggressive son Jacob. From under the shadow of the father and the son, however, there emerges a description of Isaac that reveals some qualities of character indicating that he was also a giant of a person in his own right.

Under the Shadow of Abraham (22:1 to 25:9)

Three events from the early years of Isaac are recorded in Genesis. In each of them Abraham was the central character. The record of the events was written with its focus upon the father rather than upon the son. We should remember, however, that Isaac was also personally involved in each of the incidents and that each of them had an influence upon him that helped mold his life.

The sacrifice of Isaac (22:1-19).—Abraham was confronted with a test of his faith and commitment when the call came that he sacrifice

Isaac as a burnt offering. The anguish of spirit that Abraham went through creates a dimension of deep pathos in the Genesis record.

Although Isaac was treated as a passive character in the drama, it could not have been so. The experience must have been an intense, frightening, and traumatic event in his life. He was certainly old enough to know what was going on, and he was no doubt confused by Abraham's evasive answers to his questions.

He was present when his father cut the wood that was to be used for burning the sacrifice. Later Isaac carried the wood for the fire, while Abraham carried the torch of fire and the knife for the sacrifice. The whole incident is fraught with intense emotion, for the reader can sense the puzzled mind of the lad and the anguished soul of the father. Isaac carried wood for a sacrificial fire, wondering where the sacrificial animal was. Abraham carried a knife to slay a sacrificial victim and a torch to light the fire and burn the sacrifice, knowing in his heavy heart that the planned sacrifice was his own beloved son.

The writer described the tenacious faith of Abraham in his words to the two young men who had come with them when he said, "I and the lad will go yonder and worship, *and come again to you*" (22:5). In the roll of heroes of faith, the New Testament writer of Hebrews described Abraham as one who "considered that God was able to raise men even from the dead; hence, figuratively speaking, he did receive him [Isaac] back" (Heb. 11:19).

The writer of Genesis also described the intimacy of the relationship between father and son. After leaving the servants behind, and as they went on alone toward Mount Moriah—Isaac with the wood and Abraham with the fire—"they went both of them together" (22:6). They talked about the planned sacrifice. Isaac noted that they had wood but no sacrificial animal, so he asked his father about the matter. Abraham answered that God would provide the sacrifice. He did not know how true his words were, for he fully expected Isaac to be the sacrifice.

Isaac was obviously aware of what was about to happen when he was bound and laid on the wood upon the altar. Abraham had knife in hand to slay his son before he was stopped and the ram sacrificed instead. The imprint of that frightening moment surely lived in Isaac's memory for the rest of his life. Abraham's faith had been tested and proved by this event, and the story is written from the point of view of what the experience meant to him. But the experience probably influenced the life of Isaac more than it affected Abraham. He could never have forgotten that his life belonged to God. It had been dedicated without reservation to God. Only God's gracious intervention had given Isaac back his life.

The marriage of Isaac (24:1–67).—The record of this event also has Abraham as the central character instead of Isaac. In his very old age Abraham had one last important thing to do for Isaac: to secure a wife for him. In that ancient culture it was a father's responsibility to arrange for the marriage of his children. Abraham had two deep concerns. He did not want Isaac to marry a Canaanite woman, but he did not want him to leave Canaan and go back to the land of his forefathers in search of a wife.

Abraham decided to send a servant instead to Haran to find a wife for Isaac among their kindred. As noted before, there is no indication that Ur continued to have any significant influence upon Abraham or his descendants after they left that city and migrated to Haran and Canaan. The same is not true of Haran, however. The Hebrews remembered that their history had begun in Haran and not in Canaan. Abraham and his sons remembered that their ancestral relatives were living in Haran. In order to marry within their ancestral bloodline, both Isaac and Jacob secured their wives from among those relatives living in Haran. A new Hebrew nation was founded, but some of its ties to its ancestral heritage were preserved.

At Haran the servant found Rebekah, a granddaughter of Abraham's brother Nahor. A beautiful story is told of the lovely spirit of Rebekah and of the willingness of the family for her to go away from them and be the bride of their relative.

Again, however, Isaac did not have any personal part in the drama as recorded until the very end. When Rebekah arrived, Isaac was brought into the story so they might be brought together and married. Isaac was already an adult, and he was evidently already living away from his parent's household. Abraham and Sarah had made Hebron their home before her death, and Abraham had buried her nearby. Isaac had set up his dwelling at Beer-lahai-roi in the Negeb desert to the south. He came to Hebron, where he and Rebekah met and were married.

No doubt Isaac was a more active participant in those events than the Genesis record indicates. He was not even mentioned in the ac-

count of his mother's death (23:1–20). The depth of his grief is reflected, however, in the statement that only after his marriage was
he comforted from her death (24:67). No indication is given that he
had any part in the timing or arrangement of the plans for his marriage. Yet he had come to Hebron before Rebekah arrived. He was
out in the field meditating in the evening. It seems likely that he
was anticipating the arrival of his bride, probably wondering what
she would look like and what kind of person she would be. One of
the most lovely statements in the Old Testament about husbands
and wives is written of Isaac and Rebekah: "She became his wife;
and he loved her" (24:67).

The burial of Abraham (25:7–10).—When Abraham died, Isaac and
Ishmael together buried their father at Machpelah with Sarah. That
was the first recorded meeting of the half-brothers since Ishmael and
Hager had been banished more than seventy years earlier. The story
is a record of Abraham's death. Isaac was included in the story only
as a son helping bury his deceased father. Nothing is written about
the meaning of the experience to Isaac, but surely he mourned for
his father as he had done for his mother.

A Man of Stature (25:11 to 26:35)

Genesis 25:11 indicates that the focus of covenant history would
shift to Isaac: "After the death of Abraham God blessed Isaac his
son. And Isaac dwelt at Beer-lahai-roi," an oasis south of the Negeb
near Kadesh-Barnea.[1] Isaac had already chosen that area for his dwelling before his marriage to Rebekah (24:62). It continued to be their
most settled home even though they were nomad herdsmen in desert
country. Jacob and Esau were born there and lived through their
youth years in that area. Isaac moved his basic residence later to
Gerar because of drought and famine (26:1), and later still to Beer-
sheba (26:25–33) and Hebron (35:27).

The birth of sons to Isaac (25:19–26).—Like Abraham and Sarah,
Isaac and Rebekah spent twenty childless years before they became
parents (25:20,26). At last, however, they did have twin sons. Isaac
is not described as being involved in the difficult birth or the naming
of the two sons. Because of his great love for Rebekah (24:67), however,
he must have had a great deal of solicitous concern for his wife during

the troubled pregnancy and birth. He must have been a tender man.

Rebekah went to consult a giver of oracles, probably in the sanctuary at Kadesh-Barnea or Beer-sheba, about the reason for her suffering in pregnancy.[2] The oracle she received from the Lord was that two sons were struggling within her, and their struggles were creating her difficulty. When the sons were born, Isaac and Rebekah chose names for them that seemed to fit them (see the next chapter for a discussion of the meaning of their names). The firstborn son, Esau, grew up to be a hunter, while the younger, Jacob, grew up to be a herdsman.

The parents showed obvious favoritism toward the sons, Isaac preferring Esau while Rebekah preferred Jacob (25:28). The stage was set, and resentment would surely divide Esau and Jacob and break the hearts of Isaac and Rebekah.

Isaac at Gerar (26:1–5).—Famines resulting from drought were not unusual in Canaan. During one such famine time Isaac left Beer-lahai-roi and went to Gerar. Did he go there seeking food and water, or did he go there to get on one of the caravan routes to Egypt? Whatever his intention, he did not go beyond Gerar. There he received a message from God that he was not to leave the land of Canaan, for that was to be the homeland and heritage of the covenant descendants of Abraham. The influence of Abraham's strong determination that his son not leave Canaan (24:6–8) no doubt had so conditioned Isaac that he was prepared to hear such a message from God when it came at that crucial time.

God spoke the promise of covenant blessing to Isaac. He was the son of Abraham, and God's covenant with Abraham would be continued to him. God assured him that he would have many descendants, a homeland in Canaan, and a significant place of influence and service among the nations of the world. Because Abraham had been faithful, the covenant blessing was available to his son. Isaac was called upon to stay in Canaan and fulfill the conditions of the covenant faithfully so that he and his descendants might continue to fulfill God's purpose for them.

Rebekah and the Gerarites (26:6–11).—At Gerar, Isaac used the same ruse of identifying his wife as his sister that Abraham had used with Sarah in Egypt (12:10–16) and at Gerar (20:1–18). Like Abraham, Isaac feared that he would be killed by some Gerarite who might be struck with Rebekah's beauty and want her for his harem. This incident parallels the earlier events closely enough that questions have been asked about whether three events really occurred.

There are significant differences between this incident and the ones involving Abraham and Sarah. In this case Rebekah was not taken out of Isaac's house by any of the Philistines of Gerar. In the Abraham and Sarah accounts, it was by plague and dream that the pharaoh and Abimelech became aware that Sarah was the wife and not the sister of Abraham. In this event Abimelech learned that Rebekah was Isaac's wife when he happened to see Isaac fondling her one day. Abimelech rebuked him for creating such a dangerous situation, pointing out that one of the people could easily have violated Rebekah and brought a great guilt among them (26:10). Abimelech made public the truth that she was indeed Isaac's wife and warned the people not to violate her. No major conflict arose between them as a result of the incident.

An unwelcome intruder (26:12-16).—Isaac attempted to settle down at Gerar, and that was where trouble arose between him and the people of that area. It seems they were willing to tolerate a nomad herdsman coming in to graze while drought was upon other areas, but they were not willing to have him settle down and become a farmer among them. The reference to sowing in 26:12 is the first reference to planting agricultural crops by Abraham or his descendants in the land of Canaan. This probably reflects a move by Isaac to change from the more nomadic life of a wandering herdsman to a seminomadic way of life that would include some farming and some grazing.

Isaac's clan and possessions had become quite extensive (26:14). He was not welcome as a settled resident in Gerar. They showed their lack of welcome by filling the wells that Abraham had dug earlier. The people were openly asking Isaac to move away. They feared his increasing wealth and influence.

An unwelcome neighbor (26:17-21).—Isaac moved into the region called the valley of Gerar to avoid conflict with the people. There he opened again the wells of Abraham that had been filled. He also had his workmen dig new wells. Water was vital to life, and water rights were often causes of harsh conflicts.

Isaac was not far enough away to satisfy the Gerarites; so friction continued to occur over the wells of water. Isaac named the wells Esek (contention) and Sitnah (enmity). The inhabitants were not willing for Isaac to settle in Gerar or even nearby. They would accept him peacefully only when there was distance between them.

Morality ahead of its time (26:22).—Because of the contention that did arise over the wells, Isaac gave in and moved still farther from Gerar. Isaac and his men dug another well, and that time they were far enough away from the Gerarites that they no longer objected. He named that well Rehoboth (wide places) to acknowledge that he had found enough room to live without fighting with his neighbors over the available land and water.

Isaac's actions reflect the quality of his disposition and character. He was a negotiator for peace rather than a stubborn warrior insisting upon his rights. Isaac illustrated in ancient times an application of Jesus' wise words: "If any one strikes you on the right cheek, turn to him the other also" (Matt. 5:39). He illustrated the Beatitude that the meek shall inherit the earth (Matt. 5:5). He affirmed that God had made room for us all. The earth has enough resources that we can all be fruitful in it (26:22).

Isaac and Beer-sheba (26:23–33).—Isaac chose to move again, to a place he named Beer-sheba. The Lord reassured him of covenant blessings, so Isaac built an altar and made every indication that he intended to settle there. His servants began to dig for water to supply their needs.

Abimelech came on the scene again and requested that a compact of peace be made between them. He told Isaac that he had observed God's favor upon him and that he wanted to have peace rather than a continuing struggle. Isaac was in a position to make such a covenant. He could negotiate from a position of strength and integrity, and neighborly tolerance and peace had been what he wanted all along.

They settled their agreement with an oath of covenant, and Abimelech went on his way back to his home at Gerar. Isaac's servants came with the good news that they had found water where they were digging. Then Isaac named the place Beer-sheba (well of an oath). (Note that a similar incident is reported of Abraham in Genesis 21:25–31.)

At Beer-sheba Isaac settled down and made a home. No doubt his herdsmen still ranged across the Negeb to find grazing for their cattle and sheep. But Isaac marked a distinct shift in Hebrew life from seminomad to a more settled pattern of herdsman and farmer. No record is given of how long Isaac made Beer-sheba his home. He was still living there when Jacob fled from Esau's anger (28:10), but he had moved to Hebron before the time of his death (35:27–29).

A man in his own right.—Isaac has often been described as a vital link between Abraham and Jacob, his giant father and his giant son. But Isaac was far more than a mere link. He was a significant person himself, a giant in his own right, even though he was overshadowed by his father and his son.

He did not merely walk in the continued shadow of Abraham. He established his own place as a man of stature. Isaac proved to be a skilled and diplomatic negotiator who established peaceful relations with neighboring people as he settled to live in a region near them and shared grazing areas with them.

His own family did not treat him so well, however, and the rest of the story of Isaac's life was the sad story of a good man being ill-treated by those of his own household (see Matt. 10:36).

Under the Shadow of Jacob (27:1 to 35:29)

When Isaac was a hundred years old and his sons were more than forty (see 25:26; 26:34), the focus of the family history shifted to Jacob. Isaac is described as having been old and near death (27:1–2,41), but he is nevertheless recorded to have lived another eighty years (35:27–29). Events occurred that caused the family to be shattered by a struggle for power.

Trouble in the family (27:1 to 28:9).—Jacob had already bargained Esau out of his birthright as the firstborn son of the family (25:29–34). He coveted also the father's blessing. The patriarchal blessing was a ritual in which an aging father would give the blessing of his soul to the son who would succeed him as head of the clan and carry on the family heritage.[3] That blessing by birthright belonged to Esau, and Isaac planned to bestow it on him.

Isaac instructed Esau to prepare a feast for him to provide the setting for giving the blessing. He was to hunt game and prepare a meal of savory food. No doubt he had prepared such feasts of game for his father on other occasions, and Isaac was quite fond of them. Isaac wished to be well fed and vigorous of soul when he blessed his son, for it was believed that the inner strength of the patriarch giving the blessing determined the dynamic effectiveness of the blessing he bestowed. Isaac wanted the best for Esau.

Rebekah, however, heard those instructions. Her preference for Jacob (25:28) caused her to share Jacob's covetous desire that he receive the blessing instead of Esau. Rebekah and Jacob schemed to get Isaac to bless Jacob before his plans for Esau could be completed.

Their scheme involved a quickly prepared feast and a disguise of goatskins and Esau's clothes. They were able to accomplish their deception because of Isaac's blindness. Jacob succeeded in getting Isaac's blessing bestowed on himself. When Esau returned the intrigue was exposed. Esau vowed to kill Jacob for what he had done as soon as Isaac should die (27:41). Again Rebekah learned what was about to happen, and she acted. Pretending that she feared Jacob would marry a Canaanite woman as Esau had done (26:34-35), Rebekah suggested that Isaac send Jacob to Haran to find a wife. Isaac listened to her, and Jacob was sent away.

The role Isaac played in this event is set almost into the background. He initiated the sequence of actions by his instructions to Esau about the ritual feast for bestowing the patriarchal blessing. From that point on, however, Rebekah and Jacob controlled the action that took place. Isaac and Esau are described as being outwitted and manipulated.

The price of family strife.—Isaac and Rebekah had played favorites with their sons. That favoritism finally brought havoc into the family relationships. The wife and mother became a scheming manipulator of her husband and son. Brother was divided from brother by the intense hatred that resulted. Jacob was forced to flee from home, probably never to see his mother again. No record is given of his ever being with his father again until just before Isaac's death.

Jacob proved to be the son who would carry the covenant heritage on to succeeding generations. If he and Rebekah had been of the same peaceful disposition and integrity as the meek Isaac, his place in God's purpose would surely have been fulfilled, and without the unnecessary suffering of anguish and heartache that their ambitious stratagems caused.

The death of Isaac (35:27-29).—From that point onward, the story of the covenant people became the story of Jacob and his sons. Isaac was overshadowed by this one who would eventually become Israel. But Isaac and Rebekah never knew much of the giant spiritual stature of their son.

The death of Rebekah is not recorded, but it is noted that she was buried with Isaac and the others in the cave of Machpelah near Hebron (49:31). Isaac died at age 180, after Jacob had returned from Haran. His sons, by then reconciled, buried him with his father, his mother, and his wife.

Isaac's life was one of quality and tragedy. He was a giant, but he was overshadowed by more impressive giants. He was a meek man of wisdom and integrity; but, as is often true, he was vulnerable to manipulation and abuse by others whose motives in life were less excellent. He was a man who loved deeply and suffered greatly. He was an honorable patriarch of God's people.

Notes

1. G. Ernest Wright and Floyd V. Filson, *The Westminister Historical Atlas to the Bible* (Philadelphia: The Westminister Press, 1945), p. 108.

2. Cuthbert A. Simpson, *The Interpreter's Bible* 1 (New York: Abingdon Press, 1952), p. 664.

3. Henry J. Flanders, Robert W. Crapps, and David A. Smith, *The People of the Covenant* (New York: The Ronald Press, 1963), pp. 94–95.

4. Simpson, pp. 680–681.

Jacob: Man of Action
25:19 to 50:14

The third of the Hebrew patriarchs made a mark upon their developing national history that had been preserved in the names of the tribes and the nation. Jacob became Israel. His sons became the ancestors of the twelve tribes of the Israelite nation. The story of his life is a story of struggle and intrigue, of heartbreak and hope. Sometimes he acted like a self-centered rascal. At other times he measured up to the standards of genuine greatness. He affected the course of a whole nation's life. His influence had been felt throughout most of the mideastern and western worlds.

Birth (25:19–26)

Jacob was the younger of twin sons. He and Esau were the only children born to Isaac and Rebekah. Even before these brothers were born they struggled. The word picture is that they "crushed each other" within their mother (25:22). Their struggle before birth became a foreshadowing of the conflict and rivalry in their own relationships and in that of their descendants.

Rebekah was troubled by the difficulty of her childbirth experience. She wondered if motherhood were worth the pain. Wouldn't it be better to die than to suffer as she was suffering? The message that came to her through an oracle from God was that her trouble in birth was due to the struggle of her sons. Their struggle would in time divide their descendants into two nations, and the younger brother would manipulate the older to get what he wanted. The younger son did indeed prove to be stronger and more aggressive. He did snatch away the position of heir to clan leadership. And for a time the older brother was cast into the role of servant, a role he was not willing to accept (see 27:39–40).

Esau, the older of the twins, was born red and hairy. Three names are recorded for Esau, which are all related to Esau's birth and the history of his descendants (36:8). Edom, which means red, was the name given to his descendants. Seir, which means hairy, was the name given to the land where he and his descendants lived. His personal name was Esau. That name is usually interpreted to mean hairy, but the name most likely was based on a different root word meaning to press or to squeeze.[1] The choice of the name Esau for the firstborn of the twins implied that his parents thought him to be the more aggressive of the two sons, that he had "pressed through" to be born first.

In order to get away from being subordinate to Jacob, when they were adults Esau moved to live in the region south and east of the Dead Sea. Since that area is made up largely of bare red hills, the people who lived there came to be called Edomites or "red country" people. The area came to be called Seir, "the country of the hairy man," because Esau was covered with an abnormal growth of hair over all his body. So the names recorded in relation to Esau all have significant meanings.

The name Jacob means "may God protect." [2] His parents assumed that since he was the second born, he would not be as aggressive and strong as the firstborn. They thus expected that he would need more help and encouragement and would need the Lord to protect him. He would have fewer advantages and would have to struggle more than his privileged older brother.

As the developing story of their lives indicates, these two brothers did not turn out in the ways implied by the names their parents chose for them. Esau's earlier birth was not a result of his aggressive pressing through to gain first delivery. Jacob did not accept second place or go through life needing encouragement to move out and make something of life. So another facet of meaning for Jacob's name became the one most prominently remembered.

A shorter form of the word from which Jacob's name was derived means "heel" and was used to preserve the tradition that Jacob was born holding onto the heel of Esau. That picture aptly described the way Jacob set about to "trip up" and "supplant" Esau. The name fitted him well. For much of his life he was Jacob, "the supplanter," before he became Israel, "the man who strives with God."

The Birthright Trade (25:27–34)

As Jacob and Esau grew up they developed different styles of life. Jacob became a herdsman, following the more settled life of a semi-nomad who lived in tents. His way of life was more ordered than that of Esau, who became a hunter. The hunter's life was spasmodic; he lived off the land and moved at will without dwelling or possessions to hinder. Their different dispositions increased the rivalry between them.

The birthright.—Because Esau was the older of the sons, the birthright belonged to him. It was a privileged status that went to the firstborn son in a Hebrew family. With the birthright went a double portion of inheritance in the family estate and the privilege of succeeding the father as head of the clan.

Isaac favored Esau because he was the firstborn, but Rebekah favored Jacob. Rebekah and Jacob were both jealous that the birthright privileges belonged to Esau. The parental partiality added to the problems within the family. Jacob was encouraged by his mother in his desire to supplant Esau in the foremost position in the family. Jacob obviously looked for an opportune time to make a move against his brother.

Jacob's opportunity (25:29–34).—A convenient situation arose when Jacob caught Esau in need one day. Esau had been hunting and was very hungry. Jacob had a tempting pot of soup simmering. The familiar trade took place as Esau asked for food and Jacob bargained to exchange some of his pottage for Esau's birthright. Esau reasoned that if he starved to death the birthright would be of no value to him, so he agreed to the trade.

This event reveals the character of the two young men. Jacob was envious and cunning. Esau was impulsive and concerned for the satisfaction of the moment. Jacob had accomplished one consuming desire. He had gotten Esau to swear to let him have the birthright privileges. He was only halfway to his goal, however, for Isaac was still the one who would bestow the patriarchal blessing before his death.

The Stolen Blessing (27:1–40)

Some time later the incident about the blessing occurred. Esau and Jacob were more than forty (26:34), and Isaac was becoming frail enough that he thought the end of his life was near at hand (27:1). Isaac decided it was time for him to bestow the patriarchal blessing on Esau and turn over the leadership of the clan to him. He set out the arrangements by instructing Esau in what he must do to prepare for the ceremony of the blessing. Esau was to prepare a savory meal of game he had killed. His father would take part in a ritual feast in preparation for giving the blessing. The soul of the patriarch was to be lifted to a high level of vigor, delight, and enthusiasm so the blessing he would give his son would have in it the full dynamic of his very life. Isaac told Esau to go hunt for game and begin the preparation for the blessing.

The scheme (27:5–17).—Rebekah heard Isaac as he gave those instructions to Esau. She recognized that the time for action was urgent if Jacob was to finally have the priority place in the family. She came up with a scheme by which Jacob could get to his father and receive the blessing ahead of Esau. While Esau was away on the hunt, Rebekah sent Jacob to bring two kids from the flock. With these she prepared food like that which Esau was to prepare. Her plan was for Jacob to disguise himself as Esau, take the food to his nearly blind father, and get the blessing for himself before Esau returned. Jacob had some misgivings about the scheme. After all, it would be no easy task to fool his father. Esau was his favorite son, and Isaac would surely know the feel of his hairy skin even if he did not recognize the difference in their voices. Jacob feared that he would be caught in the act of deception and receive a curse instead of a blessing. His mother persuaded him to go along with the scheme, however, and get the blessing while there was still time. Rebekah even declared that she would be willing to accept any curse that might come.

The deception (27:18–29).—Rebekah proved to be a skilled manipulator, and Jacob proved to be a persuasive liar. In the disguise of Esau's clothes, with a goatskin covering for his face and hands, Jacob deliberately told his father things that were not true and literally stole the blessing intended for the elder Esau.

Isaac questioned the quickness with which the meal had been made ready. Jacob said that God had helped him have quick success. Isaac recognized Jacob's voice but was persuaded by the disguise of goatskin that the son present was really Esau and that he had not heard correctly. Isaac then ate the ritual meal and afterward called his son to come near enough to him that he might kiss him. At that close distance Isaac recognized the smell of the field on Esau's clothes which Jacob was wearing. That was enough to convince him. He gave the patriarchal blessing to Jacob, thinking that he was blessing Esau.

The blessing involved the favor of God and the prosperity that it would bring. It involved a place of superiority over people and their subordination into a servant role. It included leadership in the clan and precedence above his brother.

The blessing once given was legally binding. It could not be revoked. It bestowed the clan headship and a double share of the family inheritance upon the one who received it. Jacob had finally gotten what he had struggled for. He had supplanted Esau and gotten for himself both the birthright and the blessing. But Esau had to be reckoned with.

Esau's anger (27:30–41).—Esau returned from the hunt with game for his father, filled with anticipation about the blessing he expected to receive. Isaac then discovered what Jacob had done. Isaac was shaken by the realization of what had happened. With forthright honesty and candor he had set into motion a plan to give the patriarchal blessing to his eldest son. But he had been deceived and tricked by his own younger son. There is no hint about whether or not he suspected the part Rebekah had played in the whole affair. He probably wondered how a person of honesty and trust could hope to protect himself from being taken advantage of by people who are willing to use fraud and cunning for selfish ends. Isaac was not a schemer; consequently, he became the victim of a wife and a son who were schemers.

Esau was bitter and asked Isaac to bless him also. Isaac's reply was that the blessing had been given already to Jacob and that nothing could change it. Jacob had been irrevocably made the head of the clan.

Esau branded Jacob with the name that really fitted him. He was indeed a "heel snatcher," one who would trip up a brother in order to gain an advantage over him. Jacob had effectively taken from him both birthright and blessing. He had thus deprived Esau of the privileges that belonged to him by customary right as the firstborn of the family. As a consequence, family relationships were shattered and deep animosities were brought to life. Esau had been cast into the subordinate role. How would he react to it?

Isaac predicted that Esau would break out of the submissive role he had been thrown into. Esau would be exiled from his home country, but he would pay that price. Esau would be a wanderer who would live off the land by his sword and would thus escape the burden of his brother.

Esau's anger was so great that he vowed he would kill Jacob as soon as their father had died. He would not bring grief to his father; but he vowed to have his revenge.

Esau the man.—No doubt the Hebrews of later generations loved these stories about Jacob and Esau. In them their ancestor had outwitted the ancestor of the Edomites, who were bitter adversaries of theirs. Esau does not show up well at all in the stories, but it may be that these narratives were somewhat unkind to him.

Esau was careless about the birthright, but not about the blessing. He was sensitive to the feelings and wishes of his aging father. Years later he proved to be noble and generous of spirit in forgiving Jacob. He was present at the death of his father to help bury him. Esau was not really a callous or uncaring person after all.

Jacob's Flight (27:42 to 29:1)

The struggle of Jacob to supplant Esau had run its course. He had gotten the patriarchal blessing. When Rebekah learned of Esau's vow of revenge, she decided that Jacob would have to leave home for a while for his own safety. As she had provided the scheme for stealing the blessing, she now devised a plan to get Jacob out of Esau's reach.

Rebekah's plan (27:42–46).—Rebekah warned Jacob of Esau's seething anger and suggested that he go to her brother Laban's house and stay for a while until Esau's rage had cooled down. Knowing Esau as she did, she expected him to forget his pique quickly. She was sure that Jacob would be able to return home safely in just a short while.

But Isaac was the patriarch, and his consent had to be given before Jacob could make such a journey. Rebekah was equal to the need of the situation. She used Esau's marriage to two Hittite women (26:34) as a reason for wanting Jacob to go away. She told Isaac that she wanted Jacob to go to her native land and seek a wife among his kin. Two objects would be accomplished by one trip, both of which were important to Rebekah. For a time Jacob could be at a safe distance from Esau, and he could find a wife for himself among his own people.

Two questions arise. Did Isaac know about Rebekah's behind-the-scenes manipulations, and did they ever have conflict over the struggle that went on in their family? It is obvious that wide differences arose between them, but there is no evidence to indicate that they ever quarreled over those differences. A second question: Did Jacob and Rebekah ever see each other again? After he left home nothing more is recorded about her until the account of her burial, which Jacob described in the third person as though he were not a part of it (49:31)

Jacob's departure (28:1–10).—Isaac took Rebekah's suggestion. He told Jacob not to marry a Canaanite woman. Since Jacob was to be the covenant line for God's people, Isaac was mindful that he should not mix their heritage by intermarriage with the Canaanites. So Jacob was sent by Isaac to Laban's clan to seek a wife.

Before Jacob left, Isaac spoke the covenant blessing upon him. He was to be God's man, and God would be the source of his strength and prosperity. The promises that had been made to Abraham and his descendants were now given to his grandson Jacob, who would carry forward God's plan for a covenant nation.

In the face of all the attention Jacob was getting, Esau tried again to please his parents by marrying one of his cousins, an Ishmaelite woman. The tragic story of family division had many dimensions. Sadness touched all their lives in unique ways.

Jacob at Bethel (28:10–22).—Jacob's journey from Beer-sheba to Haran took him along the mountain range in central Canaan. At one point he stopped for the night near a city called Luz.

Jacob was evidently exhausted from his rugged journey, for he slept on a stone for a pillow. No doubt he was lonely. Since he was separated from his mother who had pampered him, he was likely depressed also.

During that night Jacob dreamed of a ladder that reached from earth to heaven. Did that dream arise out of his longing to be in touch with something he could count on? Was the dream a message from God that the channel of communication between them was open? In the dream there came a message from God confirming the covenant between them. That was the first time Jacob had received a covenant message directly from God. God promised to protect Jacob in his travels and to bring him back safely to the land of his heritage.

When Jacob awoke he sensed that God was dealing with him. He recognized that God was present at that place; so he gave the place a name, Bethel, meaning the house of God. His reaction was in keeping with ancient Semitic conviction that some spots were especially holy.[3] Semites believed that God could be anywhere but that there were some places that he especially preferred, places where he chose to dwell.[4] If a person came to one of those places, it was especially easy to get in touch with God, for he willingly appeared to worshipers there.

It seems correct to say that the place was less important than the condition of Jacob's heart and mind. The situation that prevailed in his life created a readiness into which God could move to make himself and his will known to Jacob. The experience of that night might have happened as readily in some other place if Jacob had been there instead. It happened at Bethel, however, and the place took on great significance because of the experience he had there.

While the place may not have been as determining as Jacob believed it was, that event was very important in his relationship with God. Jacob had an awesome experience during the night. In the morning he made an altar of the stone on which he had slept, and there he made an offering in worship to God. Then Jacob made a vow. His vow was that if God would see him through his travels and help him come safely to his home again, then he would make a permanent place of worship at Bethel and give a tenth of his possessions in offering to God.

That event came at a crucial time in the life of Jacob. He was leaving home. He was out on his own. He was about to leave his homeland. It was probably the first great spiritual experience of Jacob's life. He would remember that experience, and it would influence him for the rest of his life. From Bethel he moved on toward his goal in Haran.

Jacob at Haran (29:1 to 30:43)

After Jacob arrived in the region of Haran, he came to a well and some shepherds gathered around it. Although a common situation it turned out to be a life-changing encounter for Jacob—for there he met Rachel.

When he inquired about Laban's family, Jacob was told that Laban lived nearby and that his daughter Rachel was even then coming to water his flocks at that very well. Jacob suggested that they water their sheep and move on. He implied that they should not be missing out on good grazing time. But did he really just want them out of the way so he could be alone to meet Rachel when she arrived?

Jacob's first meeting with Rachel (29:9–12).—When Rachel arrived Jacob recognized immediately that she was an extraordinary young woman. He was so excited at meeting her that by his own strength he moved a stone cover from the well which it usually took a group of men to move. Jacob made himself known to Rachel as a family kinsman, and she hastened to share that news with the rest of her family. Jacob had come to Haran to find those very relatives. It was a sign of good fortune and divine guidance that he had found them so easily.

Jacob and Laban (29:13–19).—Laban received Jacob as the kinsman he was and welcomed him into his home. Jacob stayed for a month as a guest, but a month is long enough for a visit. After that some other arrangements needed to be made. Laban said, "You don't have to work for nothing just because you're kin." Apparently that was a subtle way of saying that Laban would not support him any longer just as a guest.

Two proposals seem to have been made by Laban. One was to adopt Jacob and thus give him a formal place of belonging in the clan (note 29:14). Such adoption of a relative was not unusual in ancient Semitic culture.[5] Jacob did not seem to respond affirmatively to that proposal; so Laban then suggested that Jacob name the wages he would be willing to work for. That request opened a door for Jacob. Instead of a contract for wages, Jacob asked for the privilege of working out a dowry in order to marry the younger daughter, the lovely Rachel.

Laban was very pleased at Jacob's request. He indicated his pleasure by saying that it would be better to give Rachel to Jacob than to have her marry any other man. So Laban quickly agreed to the arrangement and sealed the bargain with Jacob.

There is rather general agreement among interpreters of this passage that the length of time Jacob was willing to serve for Rachel was quite generous.[6] Jacob was apparently willing to be generous to make sure he got what he wanted because of his great love for Rachel (29:20). Laban was pleased at the arrangement, for he could still keep Rachel in his house and continue to have her services to shepherd the flocks. He may have planned his deceptive scheme to marry Leah to Jacob even at this early stage of their contract. At the very least he would have the services of a strong and eager worker.

Jacob's marriages (29:20–30).—The agreement between Jacob and Laban was that Jacob was to work seven years as the dowry for Rachel. But the schemer Jacob had met his match in the schemer Laban. The older daughter Leah was apparently not as attractive as Rachel. Their names indicate that even at birth this difference was evident. The name Leah means cow, while the name Rachel means ewe.[7] Rachel's name was a term of endearment, for in infancy it would have meant "little ewe lamb." In addition to being less attractive, Leah is described as having weak eyes. This description may have been a reference to her appearance,[8] but more likely it means that she had limited vision. Laban must have thought that he would not be able to find a husband for Leah. So he planned a switch on Jacob.

After the seven years of service, plans for the marriage of Jacob and Rachel were made. But Laban substituted Leah for Rachel in the marriage tent. The wedding customs of that time made it possible for Laban to accomplish the deception, for the bride was brought veiled to her groom in the wedding tent.[9]

When the switch was discovered, Jacob was very angry, but he was married to Leah. There was nothing he could do about it. After his night with her in the marriage tent Jacob was legally bound to Leah Laban tried to justify his action by appealing to a custom that younger daughters were never married ahead of their older sisters. It is rather ironic that Jacob, a younger brother who "jumped ahead" of his older brother to claim a place of precedence in his family, should become victim of a custom that would not let him marry the younger daughter he loved until after the older sister was married.

Multiple marriages were acceptable, however; so Jacob demanded that Laban give him Rachel also. Laban agreed on two conditions First, Jacob must give Leah an exclusive week, for that week of the wedding feast was the usual length of festivities and was the right of every new bride. Then after his marriage to Rachel, Jacob must serve another seven years as dowry for his second wife. Jacob agreed to those terms; and after a week he married Rachel. There was never any question about which wife Jacob preferred. Rachel was his beloved, and Leah had the unenviable place of second choice. Departure from the standard of monogamy would cause heartache in that family many times.

Laban gave one maid to each of his daughters on the occasion of her wedding. Leah's maid was Zilpah, and Rachel's maid was Bilhah. The fact that he gave only one maid to each is an indication of the greedy and niggardly character of Laban. When his sister Rebekah was sent to become the wife of Isaac, she was given a nurse and several maids (24:59,61). The two maids played an important part in the history of the family, however. They became the mothers of four of Jacob's twelve sons (see 30:3–13).

Jacob's sons (29:31 to 30:24).—In the early years of his marriages, Leah was the only wife who could have children for Jacob. She gave birth to Reuben, Simeon, Levi, and Judah. The names chosen for the sons reflected the contest going on between Leah and Rachel for the place of prominence in the family. Leah was struggling for a place of established acceptance as Jacob's wife. Trying to get out of the place of unwanted second choice was a painful compulsion for her, but surely Jacob would be drawn to her since she was now the mother of his sons.

Rachel, on the other hand, was heartbroken because she could have no children. She feared that she would lose Jacob's affection. So Rachel resorted to using her servant maid to have a child for her. Bilhah gave birth to Dan and Naphtali. Rachel chose names for these sons which reflected her side of the family conflict. Leah then chose to use her maid too, since she had stopped bearing children for a time. Her maid Zilpah gave birth to Gad and Asher.

The story about the mandrakes gives an ironic side of the contest between the wives. Leah's son Reuben found some mandrakes in the field during the time of the wheat harvest. The mandrake is an herb with a tuberous root and was believed to promote conception in women. Rachel was especially interested in the mandrakes because she wanted them for herself, but she did not want Leah to have them and thus bear more children for Jacob. Rachel asked Leah for some of the mandrakes, and Leah used them to bargain for a time with Jacob ahead of Rachel. She agreed to let Rachel have some mandrakes only if she might have wifely privileges with Jacob that night. Rachel got the mandrakes that were supposed to help her conceive, but she did not have any children until years later. Leah, without the mandrakes, began to bear children again. She had two more sons, Issachar and Zebulun, and a daughter, Dinah.

At last, however, Rachel was able to have a child. She gave birth to a son named Joseph, which means "he adds." Rachel was not satisfied with one son. Now that she had borne a son, she wanted to have more children; and she expressed her desire by the name she gave to her firstborn. Joseph was the eleventh of Jacob's twelve sons. Only Benjamin, the second son of Rachel, would be born after Joseph. Benjamin was born later, after the clan had returned to Canaan (35:16–20).

Note that Levi and Judah were among the sons of Leah. They turned out to be the heads of the priestly and the messianic lines in the Hebrew nation. Joseph, the first son of Rachel, was treated by Jacob as his first true son, as though the others were not in the covenant line. This was not really different from the way Abraham set Ishmael aside and treated Isaac, his son by Rebekah, as his only true son (21:8–14). The dynamics of family conflict were growing more complex with the passage of time.

Jacob's growing wealth (30:25–43).—Jacob decided that he had served Laban long enough; so he asked his consent to leave and return to Canaan. Jacob wanted to begin accumulating some possessions for himself and his family. Laban, however, did not want him to leave. Not only would he take Laban's daughters and grandchildren with him; more importantly to Laban, his flocks had increased well while Jacob had managed them for him. He attributed his prosperity to God's blessing on Jacob. So Laban bargained with Jacob to persuade him to stay. Their agreement was a typical Oriental bargain, with each making an offer that he hoped to slip by the other. Each then planned to take advantage of the other for his own personal profit. They agreed that all the spotted and striped animals were to belong to Jacob as his wages.

Laban immediately removed all the spotted and striped stock and put them into flocks kept by his sons. That would greatly reduce the likelihood that spotted or striped young would be born in the flocks Jacob managed. But Jacob was equal to the situation and bred the strongest stock to produce striped offspring. The practice he followed was based on a widespread ancient belief that such visual impressions as Jacob used would frighten the copulating females, causing them to "mark" their offspring and bear spotted young.[10] By marking the young of the strong animals, and by letting the weaker animals breed without the striped poles before them, Jacob got the better animals and left the weaker ones as Laban's share. That time Jacob got the best of Laban in their struggle to take advantage of each other. As he increased his wealth, Jacob must have felt quite pleased with himself for having outwitted Laban and gotten even with him at last.

Time to make a move (31:1–16).—Jacob became more and more wealthy, and dangerous jealousy arose among Laban's sons. They saw their father being outsmarted and their own inheritance diminished. They did not seem to remember that most of what Laban possessed was a result of Jacob's management of the flocks during the years he had served their father (30:30). They may have been too young to have known about those earlier days, for the sons of Laban are first mentioned in 30:35. Rachel had herded the flocks before Jacob came on the scene (29:9).

Jacob became aware that Laban's attitude had changed toward him. He concluded that it was time for him to leave before trouble broke out. He felt moved by God to return to his homeland but worried about whether his wives would agree to go.

When Jacob described to Rachel and Leah the friction that had arisen between him and their father, they readily agreed to go with Jacob wherever he was inclined to go (31:4–16). They were already aware of a sense of alienation within the family. Laban had taken their dowry and used it for himself instead of making a heritage of it for them. Their future lay with their husband and children. They were ready to leave their father's clan and join their husband's people. That was a normal marriage pattern in the culture of that day.

The departure (31:17–21).—Jacob assembled his family and his flocks. They left while Laban was away shearing sheep. Before leaving, Rachel took the family household gods, small images they used in worship rituals. Possession of those teraphim would give her a legal advantage in the family inheritance. It seems likely that Rachel was interested in getting even with her father. He had robbed her at the marriage when he substituted Leah for her in the wedding. Now she would rob him by taking his household gods.

Jacob chose to leave without saying anything at all to Laban. He simply left while Laban was away. He crossed the Euphrates River and set his face to go southwest through Syria toward Canaan.

The confrontation (31:22–42).—As soon as Laban learned that Jacob had left with family and possessions, he went after them until he overtook them. The pursuit lasted seven days. Laban caught up with Jacob while he was in the hill country of Gilead, east of the Jordan River. He rebuked Jacob for leaving as he did, without giving Laban a chance to say good-bye to his daughters and grandchildren. He rebuked him also for taking the images. Jacob explained his reasons for leaving secretly, declaring that he had feared that Laban would try to forcefully prevent his family from leaving. He denied having taken the teraphim. In fact, he put his beloved Rachel in danger by vowing that whoever had taken the images would be killed.

Rachel effectively concealed the teraphim, so it appeared that Laban had no grounds for his accusation. Jacob took Laban to task harshly. He pointed out how he had brought prosperity to Laban and how he had borne the brunt of any losses in the flocks. He reminded Laban how he had served well, while Laban had changed his wages in a constant effort to deprive him of possessions he had rightly earned. Jacob attributed to God the blessings that had come to him. He declared that only God's help had enabled him to leave Laban's house without having to go away completely empty-handed. Laban had been foiled by Jacob and Rachel, and Jacob was sure that the God he had met at Bethel had helped him (see 31:13,42). No reasonable course was left except a treaty.

The watchtower compact (31:43–55).—These were, after all, Laban's daughters and grandchildren. He would certainly not be inclined to destroy them. So they made a covenant of nonviolence toward each other. They set up an altar and named the place Mizpah (watchpost). Their compact was one of nonaggression, and they called on God to watch between them as a witness to see that neither passed beyond that point to violate the agreement. Laban called on Jacob to treat his daughters well and not marry other wives. Then he bade farewell to his daughters and their children and returned home to Haran. Jacob's departure from Haran was complete. It would be permanent.

Jacob in Canaan (32:1 to 37:1)

Many changes take place in twenty years, but many things remain the same. Jacob had spent twenty years in Haran (31:38,41). He had married, begun a large family, and grown wealthy. He had not changed his scheming ways, however; nor had he done anything to heal the bad feelings between himself and Esau. As he returned to Canaan those factors would have to be dealt with.

The dread of facing Esau (32:1–21).—Before he even arrived in Canaan, Jacob sent to ask for a truce with Esau. He sent a message that he was returning to Canaan with his own servants and flocks. His message was probably meant to assure Esau that he was coming in a peaceful way, that he had his own possessions, and that he would be no threat to Esau. Jacob was evidently quite anxious about meeting Esau again. He surely remembered Esau's threat to kill him (27:41), for that was the reason he had left home twenty years before. Jacob's messengers returned with word that Esau was on his way to meet them with four hundred men. It is not a matter of surprise that Jacob was quite afraid.

Jacob did three things. (1) He divided his family and flocks into two groups so that if Esau attacked and destroyed one, the other might escape. (2) He appealed to God for help on the basis of the promises God had made to him. Jacob expressed a clear awareness of his unworthiness and of the extent of God's blessing to him. He had left Canaan alone and with nothing. He was returning to Canaan a wealthy man with many possessions and a large family. He gave God credit for his prosperity before asking his help in the meeting of Esau. (3) He sent generous gifts to Esau in the hope that he might appease him and cool his anger. Then he waited for Esau to arrive. That night proved to be a crucial night in Jacob's life.

Jacob at Peniel (32:22–32).—Jacob was camped at a ford of the Jabbok River, which flows from the east into the Jordan River a little more than halfway from the Sea of Galilee to the Dead Sea. He sent his family on across the river and stayed behind to spend the night alone. But he was not alone. God was there.

There is no actual statement as to who the "man" was who wrestled with Jacob all that night. Was it God? In naming the place, Jacob said, "I have seen God face to face." Or was Jacob wrestling with his own conscience as the Spirit of God struggled with him about the kind of person he had been all his life? The struggle reflected in the recorded dialogue is the kind of struggle a person goes through when he is trying to find out who he is with the help of the Holy Spirit.

Jacob came out of that experience a new person with a new name. At last he had faced up to the kind of person he was. A radical change took place. We could quite properly call this Jacob's conversion experience. There is no doubt that Jacob had recognized the presence of God in the struggle. He had gained new insight. He had met God in a personal experience, and the glory that belongs to God had not destroyed him (32:30). Rather, he had been preserved and sustained, and his life had been changed and enlarged.

Jacob was physically disabled by the struggle of that night. No longer would he be able to accomplish feats of physical strength such as single-handedly setting up a stone pillar at Bethel (28:18). He had a new kind of strength after the experience. A spiritual strength that came from having met God and a new strength of character caused him to be a different kind of person.

A new name was given to Jacob. He was henceforth to be called Israel, a name which means "you have striven with God . . . and have prevailed" (v. 28). New life had come through his struggle with God. So Jacob gave that place the name Peniel, a name that means the face of God. Jacob had indeed met God face to face. He could not remain the same as he was before.

After the experience of Jacob's night of wrestling with God, a new day had come to dawn. One of the most beautiful passages in Genesis describes that morning: "The sun rose upon him as he passed Peniel" (32:31). Life took on different meaning for him, as it always does when a genuine conversion takes place.

Jacob's meeting with Esau (33:1–18).—As Esau approached, Jacob arranged his family to reduce the danger to those dearest to him. The maids and their children were sent out first, followed by Leah and her children. Rachel and Joseph were placed last and farthest from any harm that Esau might intend to do. But Jacob went first of all to meet Esau and be reconciled to his brother. When they met, Jacob bowed down to the earth before Esau.

Was this conduct on Jacob's part due solely to his fear of Esau? He surely was afraid of what Esau might do to him and his family to get even for Jacob's treachery of years before. Can we not also believe that Jacob wanted a genuine reconciliation with his brother? Since his Peniel experience, we can trust that relationships with Esau were more important to him than places of priority or portions of inheritance.

Esau had not come for vengeance, however. He ran to Jacob and embraced him. An emotional reconciliation took place. Jacob presented his family and then persuaded Esau to accept the gifts he had sent to him. The events of the past appeared to have been forgotten, and everything seemed to be lovely between them. But a hint of distrust still hung like a cloud in the background. Note how it came out in their conversation.

Esau proposed that they travel together; but Jacob excused himself, saying that Esau would be hindered by the slow pace of the children and cattle. Esau then proposed to leave some of his men with Jacob (was this to keep an eye on him?), but Jacob insisted that there was no need. So Esau left and returned to his home at Seir. Jacob went on a short distance to Succoth, where he stopped for a while. Then he turned and, crossing the Jordan River, went home again into the land of Canaan. At Shechem he bought a piece of land, pitched his tents, built an altar, and worshiped God. When Abraham had arrived in Canaan on his migration from Haran, Shechem was also the first place he stopped and built an altar (12:6–7).

After his meeting with Jacob, Esau dropped out of sight. He was not mentioned again until the death of Isaac. At that time his geneal-

ogy was given and his record closed. Jacob was back in the land of
Canaan and no longer in peril from the earlier hatred of Esau; but
he was soon to learn that life among the Canaanites would not be
free from problems.

The rape of Dinah (34:1–31).—Dinah must have been no more
than a young teenager at the time. She was the seventh and last of
Leah's children and was named next to Joseph in the birth account
(30:21–24). There were only thirteen years from the time of Jacob's
marriage to Leah and the time they left Haran. Joseph was only seventeen when later he was sold by his brothers (37:2). There is, however,
no indication of the amount of time that passed between their arrival
at Shechem and this incident.

The prince of the Hivite people in Canaan, who was named Shechem, raped Dinah. Tragedy entered the relationship between Jacob's
family and the Hivites. It is to Shechem's credit that he cared enough
for Dinah that he wanted to marry her. Jacob's sons were so angry,
however, that they resorted to deceit and violence to get revenge.
They agreed for Shechem to marry Dinah only after the family of
Hamor and Shechem had all been circumcised. Their agreement was
only a trick. The agreement of the Hivites was not without selfish
motive either. They agreed among themselves to intermarry with
Jacob's clan, simply absorb them because they were few in number,
and just take over all the wealthy possessions Jacob had brought into
the land among them (34:23). With the plan for intermarriage agreed
to by both sides, the Hivite men were all circumcised. When they
were disabled by soreness from circumcision, Simeon and Levi attacked them and killed all the men in the family and plundered their
city.

Jacob rebuked his sons for what they had done. His reason for scold-
ing them was not that he disapproved of what they had done, but
that it would put him in a bad state with the surrounding people.
Jacob and his family would thus be in danger and would probably
have to move away from that area to avoid reprisal attacks. Simeon
and Levi defended their action on the basis that it was justified in
the light of what Shechem had done to their sister Dinah.

Jacob's return to Bethel (35:1–8).—When Jacob was leaving Canaan,
he had an experience with God at Bethel (28:10–19). As he returned
to the land of Canaan, God called him back to Bethel. Jacob recognized
the significance of that call. It was time for a renewal of the covenant

God had made with him years before at Bethel.

Jacob instructed his family to clear out from their lives all the pagan-ism that had become a part of them. He took all of the jewelry and other objects that had any relation to pagan religions and buried them beneath an oak tree at Shechem. A spiritual cleansing was essential to prepare for a meeting with God and a renewal of covenant.

The surrounding people were terrified of the Hebrews because of their ravage of the Hivites. So they did not dare contest their move-ment as they departed from Shechem toward Bethel. They arrived at Bethel and built an altar in preparation for the covenant renewal with God.

The death of Deborah is recorded, but there are left some unan-swered questions. When did she join Jacob's clan? Deborah was Rebek-ah's nurse and had come from Haran to Hebron with her when she came to Canaan to become Isaac's bride (24:59). Recall that Jacob was Rebekah's favorite son, so Deborah was likely very involved in looking after him when he was young. Had Rebekah died sometime earlier, and had Deborah gone from Isaac's house to become a part of Jacob's family at Haran or at Shechem? Those questions apparently must remain unanswered. Deborah was with Jacob's clan at Bethel, where she died and was buried.

God reaffirmed Jacob's new name, Israel, and renewed his covenant with Jacob and his descendants. Jacob responded by offering ritual sacrifices and recommitting himself to his covenant with God. As Pe-niel was the place of Jacob's conversion, Bethel was a place of spiritual revival.

From Bethel to Hebron (35:16–27).—On the journey from Bethel to Hebron, two things of great consequence happened. Rachel died in childbirth as Benjamin was born. Her death and burial took place at Bethlehem. Rachel called her newborn son Benoni, meaning "son of my sorrow," no doubt indicating her awareness that she was dying. Jacob gave this last son of his beloved Rachel the name Benjamin, which means "son of the south." The choice of that name for him was probably Jacob's acknowledgment that this son was born in Ca-naan instead of in the country of Haran to the far northeast, as all his other children had been. The name Benjamin could also mean "son of my right hand" (when facing east, the south is to one's right) and would have indicated how cherished Benjamin was by Jacob as his last son by Rachel.

About that time Reuben, the eldest of all Jacob's sons, seduced Bilhah. She was a concubine of his father, but she was the maid of Rachel instead of Reuben's mother, Leah. Was Reuben declaring that he, the eldest, was taking over clan leadership from his father? Was this his protest against the partiality Jacob showed to Joseph instead of to him as the eldest son? In Jacob's last blessing to his sons, he declared that Reuben was stripped of his birthright because of this incident with Bilhah (49:3–4). Through all the years, however, Jacob had not treated Reuben with the preferred status of firstborn. That preeminence in Jacob's eyes had always belonged to Joseph.

The death of Isaac (35:27–29).—Jacob moved on until he arrived again at Hebron, where Isaac was living. At age 180 Isaac died. He was buried by Jacob and Esau in the cave at Machpelah (49:31). Apparently Rebekah had already died before him, since no mention is made of her.

Esau's descendants (36:1–43).—Following the account of Isaac's death, Esau's descendants are recorded. This essentially closed the record on the Esau line, for it was the Jacob line that carried the covenant forward. Esau became the father of the Edomite nation. In his own time he became wealthy (36:7).

The sequence of Esau's residence movements is not altogether clear. He was apparently living in the region near Hebron at the time Jacob stole the patriarchal blessing (27:1 ff). When he met Jacob in Gilead and they were reconciled, Esau's main residence was identified as Seir (33:16). In this account of his genealogy, Esau and Jacob are described as dividing the land because of their vast herds, as Abraham and Lot had done (compare 36:6–7 with 13:6–9). It seems that while Jacob was in Haran, Esau may have ranged his herds from Hebron to Seir in search of grazing. After Jacob's return to Hebron, they evidently agreed that Jacob would graze the Hebron region and Esau the Seir region. Such an agreement would reduce the likelihood that their herdsmen would conflict over grazing and water. Though they were kindred, bitter rivalry and often open hostility prevailed between the descendants of Esau and Jacob. Their agreement to divide the land for living and grazing did not prevent times of conflict in succeeding generations.

Sorrow returned (37:1–36).—Trouble broke out in Jacob's family. The jealousy between Rachel and Leah erupted into strife again in their children. Jacob's obvious preference for Joseph was part of the

unwholesome environment in the family (37:3–4). Joseph's egotism
added to the problem. All these factors led to a cruel act by the
older brothers.

They stripped Joseph of his long coat to show their scorn for the
favored treatment he received from their father. Joseph was sold as
a slave to get him out of the way. Jacob was deceitfully led to believe
that Joseph had been killed by a wild animal (37:31–33).

The record of this event is something of a summary, for through
this incident Joseph was brought to the forefront and Jacob moved
into the background. Though this is described as "the history of the
family of Jacob" (37:2), the focus is upon Joseph; and the biblical record
henceforth was made up primarily of "Joseph stories." Jacob was at
last established again in the homeland of his fathers. His own family
was in open conflict as a result of the competition and friction between
the parents in the early years of the children's lives.

Heartbreak came to Jacob when Joseph was taken from him. His
beloved Rachel and her firstborn were both now gone from him. It
was as though joy had gone out of his life.

Trouble plagued the family (38:1–30).—The incident of Judah and
Tamar illustrates the ancient idea that people live on in their children.
When a man died childless, his nearest kin was to produce a child
by the widow to be as an offspring for the deceased.[11] By the family
customs of the time, Judah was obligated to give first Onan and then
Shelah to Tamar, the wife of Er, as husbands so that descendants
might be born to carry on the name of their deceased brother Er.
Onan's unwillingness to father a child for his deceased brother led
to his own death, and Judah was then unwilling to give Shelah to
Tamar for fear that he would suffer the same fate.

Tamar later chose to expose Judah's failure to keep faith with her
by tricking him into fathering a child by her. Judah fell into her trap,
and the outcome was that Judah confessed that he had violated an
established custom.

This story tells of evil, contempt, fear, and deceit within Judah's
family. The incident is an example of the trouble that plagued Jacob's
family. The sinfulness of many years kept paying off in bitter fruit.

Jacob had met God at Peniel and had become a new man. The
influence of his earlier life lingered on within his family, however,
and much sorrow came as a continuing effect of a self-centered past.

Not even being God's covenant people or living in the land of Canaan exempted Jacob's family from the consequences of humanness and sin.

Jacob in Egypt (42:1 to 50:14)

Joseph rose to prominence in Egypt, and he was in a position to help his father's family when need arose. And need did arise. A famine developed in Canaan, but Joseph had supervised the storage of great grain reserves in Egypt. As often happened in Canaan, the people had to look to Egypt for food in time of famine. In that way Joseph and his brothers met again.

Jacob was quite willing for ten of his sons to travel to Egypt to buy grain for the clan (42:1–3; 43:1). He was staunchly unwilling for Benjamin to go, however (42:4, 34–38; 43:3–6). Rachel and Joseph had already been taken from him, and Simeon was a hostage in Egypt. Jacob was afraid something would happen to Benjamin if he were to go on a trip to Egypt. The other sons had learned to live with the fact that Benjamin was Jacob's protected favorite. They might resent it, but that was how it was in the family.

Only as a last resort, when their food was almost gone and the other sons refused to go without him, did Jacob agree for Benjamin to go. Reuben, the eldest, offered to guarantee Benjamin's return with the life of his own two sons (42:37), but Jacob would not accept his promise. (Was Jacob still distrustful of Reuben because of the incest with Bilhah? See 35:22.) Judah later came forward and offered to be personally responsible for Benjamin's safe return (43:8–11). Only then did Jacob agree for him to go.

The drama in Egypt was played out between Joseph and his brothers. After he finally identified himself to them and was reconciled with them, his immediate concern was to arrange for his father and all the clan to come to him in Egypt. When the sons arrived back in Hebron and told Jacob that Joseph was alive, he was simply overwhelmed. Those words were incredible. The news was too good to be true. Only the sight of the wagons that had been sent to transport them to Egypt was sufficient to convince him that it was all really true. Then he had no difficulty in making a decision. His firm and resolute word was "I will go and see him before I die" (45:28).

Jacob and his clan migrated to Egypt to be with Joseph so he could take care of them. The account of their movement to Egypt includes the whole clan, but it was basically a "Joseph" story; he was the central figure.

Leaving his homeland again (45:27 to 46:7).—Before Jacob left the land of Canaan, he stopped at Beer-sheba and offered sacrifices (46:1). That site had been the home of his father Isaac for a time (26:23–25), and it was Jacob's boyhood home (28:10). He evidently had some misgivings about leaving Canaan even though he longed to go to Joseph. Assurance from God gave him permission to go (46:2–5).

God promised Jacob two important things that became the basis of his assurance that it was right for him to go to Egypt. God identified himself as the covenant God of Abraham and Isaac, and he promised Jacob that the covenant would hold for him even while he was in Egypt. In leaving Canaan he would not sever the covenant between them. The promise that Jacob would be made a great nation would go on being fulfilled in Egypt (46:3). God also promised Jacob that he would go to Egypt with him and later help him return to Canaan (46:4).

Ancient peoples identified their deities with a defined local area. A certain land was where a god had dominion, and that land was where that god would abide. Jacob thought of Canaan as God's land; so to leave Canaan would mean to him that he was going away from the place where God dwelt, away from the place where he could hope for help from God. For that reason, God's promise to go with him to Egypt was an unexpected promise of good fortune and blessing to Jacob.

They came to Egypt (46:26 to 47:12).—When Jacob and his family arrived in Egypt, Joseph arranged for them to settle in the land of Goshen. In that area they would enjoy good grazing for their flocks. They would also be somewhat separated from the Egyptian people, which would reduce the likelihood of friction between them (47:3–6).

At that period in history the Egyptian capital was Avaris, a city in the lower Nile delta region. By settling the clan in Goshen, Joseph kept them near enough to him that he could be their protector.

Jacob was 130 years old when he went to Egypt, and he lived in Egypt for seventeen years before his death (47:28).

Jacob's death (47:29 to 50:14).—Before his death Jacob did two things. He insisted that Joseph promise not to bury him in Egypt. Jacob wanted to be buried in his homeland, in the burial ground at Hebron with his ancestors (47:29–31).

Jacob also gathered his sons around him and gave to each a blessing before he died. He showed great insight into the personal qualities of each of his sons. His words were indeed prophetic, but he also spoke of traits that had already shown up in their lives. What they would become could already be seen in what they were.

After Jacob's death, Joseph arranged for a funeral migration to take him to Hebron for burial at nearby Machpelah. Then Joseph and the Hebrew clan returned to Egypt and to Goshen.

Joseph was unquestionably established as the clan head. Jacob had always treated him in a special way because he was Rachel's firstborn.

At Jacob's death he left the clan and the covenant to Joseph (49:22–26). He had snatched the birthright from Esau by deceit; but he would not give the blessing to Reuben, who had tried to displace his father before his death (35:22; 49:3). After a life of action, Jacob left the leadership of his clan to Joseph, who was "a fruitful bough by a spring" (49:22).

Notes

1. Clyde T. Francisco, *The Broadman Bible Commentary* 1 rev. (Nashville: Broadman Press, 1973), p. 200.

2. Charles M. Laymon, ed., *The Interpreter's One-Volume Commentary on the Bible* (New York: Abingdon Press, 1971), p. 20.

3. Cuthbert A. Simpson, *The Interpreter's Bible* 1 (New York: Abingdon Press, 1952), p. 689.

4. Frederick C. Eiselen, Edwin Lewis, and David G. Downey, *The Abingdon Bible Commentary* (New York: Abingdon Press, 1929), p. 238.

5. John Bright, *A History of Israel* (Philadelphia: The Westminster Press, 1972), p. 78.

6. Gerhard von Rad, *Genesis* (Philadelphia: The Westminster Press, 1976), p. 290.

7. Ibid., p. 291.

8. Ibid.
9. Simpson, p. 700.
10. Von Rad, pp. 301–302.
11. Ibid., p. 358.

Joseph: Man of Service
30:22 to 50:26

The record of Joseph's early years is sketchy. He is referred to only twice before the family moved from Haran to Canaan, but those references are very enlightening.

Joseph was the firstborn son of Rachel; and as such he had a special place in his father's affections because Rachel was Jacob's favorite wife. The genuine love he had for her was beautiful, but it was also a source of jealousy and trouble in the family. Joseph was caught up in that family struggle from his very birth.

Rachel and Leah were in fierce competition for Jacob's affection. The birth of Joseph brought a significant change into the family situation. Previously Leah had borne six sons and a daughter, while Rachel had been childless. Now Rachel also had a son. She chose the name Joseph for him. Two possible meanings of that name are recorded. One form of the root word from which the name was likely derived means to take away, while another root form means to add to.[1] Both ideas are preserved in the text, and both had special meaning to Rachel when Joseph was born.

The birth of a son did "take away" her reproach and relieve the sense of shame she had suffered though the years when she had been childless (30:23). She desired more children to fulfill her maternal longing and to strengthen her position as Jacob's wife. So the birth of one son, Joseph, stirred in her heart the hope that God would "add to" her another son. The biblical text gives greater weight to her expressed hope that God would enable her to have more children (30:24).

Joseph was evidently not yet a teenager when Jacob left Laban's house to migrate back to Canaan. All of Jacob's children except Benjamin were born between the seventh and the fourteenth years of the stay in Haran (compare 29:20; 30:25–26). They stayed in Haran for another six years before leaving for Canaan (31:41).

The next reference to Joseph, after the record of his birth, is his appearance in the story of Jacob's reunion with Esau.

Jacob expected Esau still to be violently angry about the trickery he had played in robbing him of the blessing of the firstborn. Esau had vowed that he would kill Jacob for what he had done (27:41); so as Jacob drew near to Canaan, he became more and more afraid of what Esau might do to him and his family.

Jacob planned a strategy to reduce the damage Esau might do. He sent gifts on ahead to Esau. Then he arranged his possessions so Esau would meet only one group at a time. If Esau attacked one group, the others would stand a better chance of escaping. In all his planning Jacob placed Rachel and Joseph last and farthest from Esau so they would face the least possible danger (33:2,7). In that incident Jacob showed again his partiality for Joseph over the other sons, a favoritism that caused much heartache in the family.

Joseph and His Brothers: Conceit and Jealousy (37:2–36)

After being reconciled with Esau and stopping for a while at Shechem, Jacob returned to Hebron and settled in the region that had been home to Abraham and Isaac. The clan followed the established seminomad pattern of sheepherding. Jacob's sons moved with the flocks to scattered grazing areas. Sharp jealousy developed among them because of Jacob's special treatment of Joseph (37:3–4). That ill will was increased when Joseph made bad reports to his father about the brothers. The text does not indicate whether they were lazy and did not do their work well, or whether their attitudes of resentment toward Joseph were the things he reported. To the brothers, Joseph was a despised, spoiled tattler.

The jealousy was keenest on the part of the four sons of Bilhah and Zilpah (37:2; see 35:25–26). No doubt those sons, being children of the servant concubines, had the lowest rank within the family and resented the discrimination. Joseph's place as the favored son was reflected in the long robe Jacob provided for him The ordinary tunic was sleeveless and reached only to the kees. It therefore gave freedom of movement to both arms and legs as a person worked.[2] Joseph's robe was long, probably reaching down to the soles of his shoes; and it had long sleeves also. This type of robe indicated that Jacob intended for Joseph to be the "gentleman son," not a worker with the sheep as the other sons would be. Joseph would be Jacob's right-hand man, staying close to home with his father and learning from the involvements of being head of the clan. It is not surprising that the other sons were offended by such obvious and blatant favoritism.

The description of Joseph as "the son of his [Jacob's] old age" (37:3) is difficult to understand. Jacob was somewhat over forty when he stole the patriarchal blessing and fled to Haran (see 26:34). Joseph was born before the end of his fourteenth year in Haran (see 30:25–26); so Jacob was not more than sixty when Joseph was born. Their return to Hebron and the birth of Benjamin both occurred before Joseph was sold into slavery at age seventeen. Benjamin was consequently born before Jacob was eighty. Benjamin also is described as a son of Jacob's old age (44:20). But Jacob lived to age 147 (47:28); so neither of these sons were born when he was in the latter years of his life.

Note, however, that the text does not require these descriptions to be references to their time of birth. In both instances the reference may well be to each of the sons' relationship to his father. Before he was sold into slavery, Joseph was the son on whom Jacob centered the focus of his hope for the future. This was the son who was dearest to his heart, the one he would keep close to him, the one to whom he would give the patriarchal blessing and the headship of the clan. Joseph was the son to whom Jacob would cling in his old age. Through this most cherished son Jacob would hope to have his dreams for the future fulfilled. After Joseph was sold into slavery and Jacob thought he had been killed, Benjamin took the place of precedence with his father. He became the "son of his father's old age," the one he expected would give assurance and hope to his last years.

The pampered dreamer (37:5–11).—Jacob's special treatment of Joseph caused the other sons to be jealous and resentful. Joseph became conceited. His egotism was reflected in two dreams. His first dream was about sheaves of grain. As he and his brothers were binding sheaves, their sheaves bowed down around his sheaf. His second dream was of the sun, moon, and stars bowing down before him. Joseph was so indiscreet that he told the dreams to his family, and the jealousy within the family increased.

Some indication of destiny was revealed in Joseph's dreams. Years later in Egypt both his brothers and his father did bow before him. He became a high official in Egypt, and during the famine years they became subject to his authority in their need for food. At the time of the dreams, however, there was no indication that any member of the family understood the dreams to have any element of divine revelation. Joseph made no claim that God had spoken to him. He only reported that he had dreamed these dreams. The brothers were even more offended by Joseph's obvious sense of self-importance. Jacob was also struck by this evidence of his son's exalted ego. It made him wonder what that development might mean (37:11).

Only at a much later time, when the dreams actually came true and destiny was realized, did they see the prophetic element in them (42:6; 47:11–12; 50:18). Until then the dreams were seen as mere expressions of Joseph's exaggerated egotism. They caused increased ill will between him and his brothers.

Victim of vengeance (37:12–36).—Joseph's brothers took their father's flocks to graze in the region near Shechem, about fifty miles north of their home at Hebron. After some time Jacob sent Joseph to see how the brothers and sheep were getting along. In the meantime they had moved with the flocks to Dothan, some fifteen miles farther north. Joseph found them there, but he was very unwelcome when he arrived.

The brothers remembered the tales he had carried to their father about them (37:2). They were still smarting from his conceited dreams (37:19). They conspired to kill him and get him out of their lives. That would put an end to his haughty ways. Reuben, the eldest, had a cooler head, however, and a sense of responsibility. He suggested that they not kill Joseph but just pitch him into a dry pit in the wilderness and let him die. That would get rid of him without their actually killing him. The others went along with Reuben's suggestion. He intended to get Joseph out of the pit later and send him away to keep the brothers from doing violence to him. Sometime later, before Reuben had a chance to rescue Joseph, a different turn of events took place.

As the brothers were sitting together and eating, a caravan of Ishmaelite traders came by on their way to Egypt. The names Ishmaelite and Midianite seem to have been used interchangeably (37:25,28,36; 39:1), or else two caravans were involved. They regularly trafficked in slaves, and Judah thought of a way the brothers could make some money. Instead of killing Joseph, he suggested that they sell him to the traders. They could make a profit and get rid of Joseph at the same time. Joseph was sold for twenty shekels, and the traders took him to Egypt with them. Apparently Reuben was not with them at the time of the sale. When he later returned to the pit and found Joseph gone, he was very upset; but there was nothing he could do.

They took Joseph's long coat, soaked it in blood, and sent it home to their father. There is no indication of whether one of the sons took the coat or whether they sent a servant on that cruel errand. They asked Jacob to identify the coat, saying that they had found it. Jacob concluded that Joseph had been killed by a wild beast of some kind and eaten. Jacob was heartbroken and mourned for Joseph a long time, not dreaming that he was alive in Egypt. The sons joined the rest of the family in trying to comfort Jacob in his grief. What duplicity!

Two strokes of irony are included in this event. Reuben was the eldest son of Jacob, but his mother was Leah; so he was denied the place in his father's affection that a firstborn son usually had. Throughout his life he had been treated like a second-class person in contrast to Joseph, the firstborn of Rachel. Reuben had further alienated himself from his father by his violation of the concubine Bilhah (35:22). He had been thoroughly displaced by Joseph. Nevertheless, he was a decent enough person to rise above his own humiliation and illtreatment to rescue Joseph from the hatred of the other brothers. Reuben persuaded them not to destroy the very person who had the place of status in the family that normally would belong to him.

A second notable aspect of this event has to do with the sons' deception toward their father. Years before, Jacob had deceived his father Isaac and robbed him of the privilege of bestowing the patriarchal blessing on his favorite son Esau as he had planned to do. Now Jacob was deceived by his sons as they deprived him of his favorite son and tricked him into believing that Joseph had been killed. Reuben rose above the temptation to destroy his despised younger halfbrother, but years of family dissension still brought cruel sadness to the troubled clan.

Meanwhile Joseph had been sold to Potiphar, an Egyptian military official. The anger of the brothers had finally gotten its vengeance. They thought they were finished with Joseph forever.

Joseph's Servant Years in Egypt (39:1 to 41:36)

A whole new world opened for Joseph. Instead of being the favored son in the house of his father Jacob, he was a slave in the house of a foreigner. But Joseph proved to be a person of ability and integrity by the way he adapted to his new role in life. New traits of character surfaced in him. His former egotism gave way to an appropriate humility. Mature responsibility and moral uprightness were clearly manifested. He did not have an easy life any longer, but he measured up and proved to be a person of real stature in whatever circumstances he was found.

Learning servanthood (39:1-23).—God helped Joseph, and he was successful in doing the things assigned to him. Potiphar noticed the kind of person Joseph was and the effective quality of his work. So Potiphar advanced him to the position of overseer. As such he was in charge of Potiphar's household operation, and he had his master's complete confidence (39:6). But danger lurked ahead.

Joseph was handsome, and Potiphar's wife became infatuated with him. She attempted to seduce Joseph into a sexual affair, but he had too much moral integrity to fall for the temptation. He insisted that it would be unthinkable to violate the trust of his master and do such a sinful thing. Potiphar's wife persisted and became more aggressive until one day he had to strip off his coat to escape from her grasp.

Her anger at being rejected was so great that she turned on Joseph and accused him of trying to attack her. She made that vicious charge to the household servants and later to her husband. Normally a slave so charged would have been killed immediately; but in spite of his anger, Potiphar only threw Joseph in prison.[3] One wonders if Potiphar suspected what had really happened.

Joseph's ability showed itself soon in the prison. With God's help he rose to responsible assignments. Eventually he was put in charge of the prison operations. He had learned to serve and to lead. He was put into places where his future would be influenced. God was surely opening a way for Joseph's future role as his servant in Egypt.

Interpreter of dreams (40:1 to 41:36).—Two of the king's servants, the chief butler and the chief baker, were in the same prison with Joseph. No indication is given of the nature of their offenses or of why the king was angry with them. They were both put into his charge. Joseph's dreams had gotten him into trouble as a lad. Now his interpretation of dreams became the means for his being freed from prison and raised to prominence. The hand of God was present in all of these happenings, for Joseph believed that God was the source of his dream interpretation (40:8).

The butler and baker both dreamed and were disturbed when they could find no one in the prison to interpret their dreams. If they had not been confined to prison, they would have gone to the professional dream interpreters to learn the meaning of their dreams. Since they could not, they were downcast and troubled. Joseph declared that God would give them an interpretation, and he volunteered to be their interpreter.

The butler's dream was of a vine with three branches that blossomed and bore clusters of ripe grapes. He then pressed the grapes into the king's cup and gave it to him. Joseph interpreted the dream to mean that in three days the butler would be released and restored to his place of service as the cupbearer for the king. He asked the butler to put in a good word for him with the pharaoh, to help Joseph gain his release from prison since he was innocent of any wrongdoing.

Since the butler's dream had a favorable interpretation, the baker decided to let Joseph interpret his dream also. His dream was of three cake baskets that he carried on his head. The top basket was filled with all sorts of baked food that he was taking to the king, but birds were stealing the food from the basket and eating it. Joseph interpreted the baker's dream to mean that within three days he would be executed by hanging. In a short time both dreams turned out as Joseph interpreted them. The baker was executed, and the butler was restored to his former official place.

Joseph had asked the butler to make a plea for him to the king (40:14), but after his release the butler forgot about him (40:23). So for two more years Joseph stayed in the prison. His ability to interpret dreams would still benefit him, however, for the king was also a dreamer.

The king dreamed of seven fat cows being devoured by seven lean cows. He had a second dream of seven full heads of grain being swallowed up by seven thin heads of grain. The double qualities convinced him that the dreams had special meaning and would certainly come to pass. No Egyptian wise man or magician could be found who could interpret the pharaoh's dreams, so he was distressed. Then his butler remembered how Joseph had interpreted his dream correctly, so he mentioned it to the king. Joseph was brought from the prison to the king to interpret his dreams.

The injustice of his years in prison and the discouragement of having been forgotten by the butler had not broken Joseph's spirit or caused him to lose his faith. When he was summoned to appear before the pharaoh, Joseph shaved according to Egyptian custom and changed his clothes. He had pride in his appearance, and he wished to make a favorable impression on the king.

Joseph was brought into the presence of the king, who told him that he had dreams he wanted Joseph to interpret. Joseph insisted again that he could not interpret dreams but that God could; and he said he would give the king an answer to the meaning of his dreams. The king told his dreams to Joseph, and he interpreted them to be a warning from God that seven years of famine would follow seven years of abundant harvests. The blighted years would use up all that could be gained in years of plenty. Joseph suggested that a manager of grain supplies be appointed and that reserves from the good years be stored for the time of the famine to come. He specified that a fifth of each plentiful harvest should be set aside for food and seed for the famine years.

At last Joseph had come to the attention of the king. His ability to interpret dreams had brought him before the king in a favorable light. The situation turned out well for Joseph and for all the people of the land.

Joseph in the Pharaoh's Court (41:37–57)

The king was impressed by Joseph's dream interpretation and by the wise suggestion he had made about storing grain reserves. He recognized the guiding inspiration of God in the life and counsel of Joseph, so he appointed him to be the official who would do what he had suggested.

The pharaoh established an official position for Joseph and gave him great authority. The ring, linen robes, gold chain, and reserved place in the second chariot were all symbols of the high rank of his position. Joseph was second in authority only to the king himself. The signet ring that Joseph wore enabled him to make laws in the land just as the king did. In ancient times the king stamped official documents with a ring on which his personal seal was engraved. Joseph was given authority to "sign the king's name" on official orders.[4] He was given complete control over the affairs of the nation (41:44).

Joseph was given a new name to fit his new position. The name Zaphenath-paneah means revealer of secrets. Thus Joseph was recognized for interpreting the king's dreams and for suggesting a way to deal with the great national need ahead. Joseph was also given an Egyptian wife named Asenath. He was raised to a place of established leadership and prominence. He was in a position where he could serve God, his family, and the Egyptian people by avoiding great suffering and widespread starvation. At age thirty this young Israelite was in one of the most crucial places of leadership, influence, and service in all the history of mankind.

During seven years of abundant harvests, there was plenty of food throughout Egypt. Joseph supervised the gathering into reserve storage all the available surplus. The grain was stored in all the cities throughout the land. In each city the grain was stored from the surrounding region. So much was gathered into storage that they had no record of the total amount.

Those were good years in Egypt. They were good years for Joseph, too. Two sons were born to him and Asenath. Their firstborn was named Manasseh, which means "making me forget." No indication is written that Joseph was longing for his family and home in Canaan. However, this choice of a name for his son would suggest that the joy of having a son was indeed helping him overcome any homesickness he had for his father's house.

The second son of Joseph and Asenath was named Ephraim, which means fruitful. This choice of name for a second son suggests their joy at the fruitfulness of having another child. The name also suggests that Joseph was occupied in those years with concern about the fruitfulness of harvests and the growing grain reserves.

After the seven years of full harvests, droughts came; and famine developed throughout Egypt. Joseph then began to sell the stored grain to the people. People from other nations also came to Egypt to buy grain. Egypt was the main source of grain in the ancient Middle East. The annual overflow of the Nile River caused Egypt to have more dependable harvests than any of the surrounding nations. When Egypt had drought, it was almost certain that everybody else in that part of the world would have drought also. The Egyptian grain reserves were vital to the people of that nation. They were also vital to Joseph's family in Canaan.

The Israelite Migration to Egypt (42:1 to 47:12)

When the famine became severe in Canaan, the people turned to Egypt in search of grain for food. Jacob sent ten of his sons to make a journey to Egypt and bring back food for the clan. He would not consent for Benjamin to go. After all, Rachel had died and Joseph was believed to be dead; so Benjamin was all that Jacob had left of that part of his family. The ten brothers apparently went along with a caravan of others who were going to Egypt on a food-buying mission also (42:5).

Joseph and his brothers (42:6–28).—Because of his position, Joseph was responsible for the distribution of grain from the reserves to the Egyptian people during the famine. He was also in charge of approving foreign traders who came to buy grain. It was thus that Joseph and his brothers met again for the first time since they sold him into slavery some twenty years before. He recognized his brothers when they came before him to be approved to buy grain, but he did not give any indication that he knew who they were. They did not recognize him, however; and it is not surprising that they did not. Years had passed. Joseph had become an adult, and he was dressed as an Egyptian official. No one would ever have dreamed that this influential official was the same person they had sold as a lad to the Ishmaelite traders.

They bowed before Joseph. They were in the presence of an impressive and powerful dignitary. Oriental court customs required that they show respectful deference to him. They also wanted to impress him favorably because they wanted his approval to buy food. As they bowed before him, Joseph was reminded of the dream he had had as a lad (37:6–8). The brothers had been incensed by his egotism then, and they had done everything they could to thwart the fulfillment of his dream. When their anger was great enough that they planned to kill him, their vengeful thought was, "We shall see what will become of his dreams" (37:20).

Destiny had turned the tables. Years before, Joseph had been in their hands and subject to any savage revenge they might take upon him. Now they were in his hands and subject to whatever cruelty or kindness he would show to them. Joseph's dream had come true. His brothers were bowed before him. He had not forced them to do so. Circumstances had led them to make that choice, though they were unaware that the man before whom they knelt was Joseph.

All the foreigners who came to Egypt to buy grain were examined carefully to guard against spies. Concern about invasion from the direction of Canaan was a characteristic feature of Egyptian life during those centuries.[5] The powerful empires of that era were around the fertile crescent from Egypt, through Canaan and Syria, to Assyria and Babylon. That period saw the migration of the Asiatic Hyksos into Egypt. The threat of invasion was felt keenly during the years of the famine. They feared an adversary would take advantage of the weakened condition of the land and launch a military expedition against them to conquer the nation or to raid their crucial grain reserves (42:9).

Joseph was harsh with his brothers and accused them of being spies. He seems to have been testing them, however, rather than trying to bring vengeance upon them (42:15–16). But what was Joseph testing? He recognized his brothers, and he surely knew that they were not spies. Their clan could have presented no threat to the might of Egypt, even in a famine time. Nor did he need to test them to know the truthfulness of the information they gave about their family. He knew as well as they about the younger brother at home with the father, and he knew of the one "who is no more"—their reference to Joseph himself (42:13). The crux of the test lay in Joseph's words "whether there is truth in you" (42:16). His intention was to find out what kind of persons they were.

In response to Joseph's questions, they freely gave information about their family to try to prove their trustworthiness. Thus Joseph was able to learn about his father and brother without revealing who he was. He also set the stage for learning whether these brothers were really as loyal and unselfish as they presented themselves to be. Had positive changes really taken place in their lives? Joseph would find out.

He proposed to hold hostage all but one, who was to go and bring Benjamin to Egypt to prove the truth of their story about who they were. They were then kept in prison for three days, apparently to impress upon them how serious their situation was. After that Joseph sent for them and told them he would keep only one hostage while the others took food home to their hungry families.

The guilty consciences of the brothers began to trouble them, for they considered their ill fortune to be a consequence of what they had done to Joseph years before (42:21–22). He had said nothing to imply that there was any relationship between his treatment of them and anything they had done in the past. Their bitter self-recrimination revealed a strong moral tone of life among the Israelites. They believed that when evil was suffered it was related to evil that had been done, and they knew in their hearts that they had done wrong in their cruel vengeance against Joseph.

They had no idea, however, that Joseph was understanding every word they said when they talked about those events of time past. Reuben reminded the other brothers of his warning not to do what they had done. He recalled how he had had no success in stopping their drive to get rid of Joseph and how they were all reaping the moral consequences of the evil. Joseph learned from their conversation, probably for the first time, that Reuben had come to his defense years before and had tried to prevent what had happened to him. No doubt his personal feeling toward his older half-brother changed greatly at that moment. He was so moved by what he heard that he left their presence and wept.

A single hostage was then chosen. Joseph took Simeon and bound him as a prisoner before the brothers. They were to be left with no question that Joseph meant what he said when he told them to bring Benjamin back to prove their honesty. But why Simeon? Two reasons. Reuben had just gained a favorable place with Joseph by his innocence in regard to the sale into slavery. At the same time Reuben, while he was the eldest son, did not have a high standing with Jacob because of the Bilhah incident (35:22). Simeon was the next oldest brother, and he would be looked upon as responsible for the conduct and safety of the group while they were away from home.

Joseph then ordered that their bags be filled with grain. He also instructed that their money be placed secretly in the bags to be found later, probably back at home, for provisions were given to them for the journey. So they departed for home with their supplies of grain.

After a day's journey, when they stopped for the night, one of them discovered his money in a bag of grain. Though they were innocent,

they thought they were really in trouble. They felt they would surely
be accused of stealing the money. They considered this additional
misfortune to be further punishment for their former evil.

A question about motivation needs to be considered here. Why
did Joseph have the money returned to his brothers secretly in the
bags of grain? Was it an act of generosity on his part, indicating his
intention to give his family the food they needed? Or was it a planned
way of striking additional fear in their hearts through the probability,
which they would think certain, that they would be accused of stealing? Both motives were possible, but Joseph's overall conduct indicates
he most likely intended a free gift to reduce the costs of the famine
to his family. In fact, however, the outcome was an intensification
of the fear his brothers experienced. Their deep sense of guilt caused
them to see the dark side of everything that was happening to them.

Another question should be asked about where the money was discovered. One of them found his money after a day's travel (42:27),
but why would he have opened the grain bags packed for travel since
provisions for the trip were furnished to them (42:25)? When they
opened the bags at home and found money in them, they were dis-
mayed as though they had known nothing about it until then (42:35).
On their second trip to Egypt, they recounted the incident to Joseph's
personal steward and reported that they had found all the money
at the lodging place after the first day of travel (43:21). The three
references, taken together, seem to imply that one brother discovered
his money and the others searched and found theirs also. But on
arriving at home they made no mention of it to Jacob and appeared
to be surprised when it was discovered. Perhaps they wanted to avoid
Jacob's criticism for carelessly letting the family be put in such a
hazardous situation. After all, they had enough other bad news to
report to him.

Back at home (42:29 to 43:15).—When Jacob's sons arrived home
in Hebron, they told their father all about the events of the trip.
They told him how Simeon had been kept hostage until they could
prove that they were trustworthy and not spies. They reported Joseph's demand that Benjamin be brought back to Egypt to prove
their truthfulness before Simeon would be released. Without that they
would be permitted to buy no more grain.

Then they opened the bags with the money inside, and the whole
affair became more involved and incredible. What in the world could

they do? Could they dare return to Egypt after having brought the money back with them? But how could they not go to secure the release of Simeon? Would they simply forsake him?

Jacob was not willing to let Benjamin go to Egypt. He was caught in a terrible dilemma. Reuben promised to be personally responsible for Benjamin's safe return, but that did not gain any approval from Jacob. He apparently was not convinced that Simeon's release could be gained anyway. He counted the risk too great to agree for Benjamin to go.

Only after food became very scarce could Jacob be persuaded to let Benjamin go to Egypt. He suggested that the other sons go without him, but they refused to do that. Jacob came very close to accusing the sons of bringing this sadness on him by telling that he had a son at home (43:6). They replied, and truthfully so, that they were innocent, for they had only answered the questions of Joseph honestly. And he was the official who must approve them for buying grain, so they could not very well decline to answer his questions. They had intended no ill to their father or their younger brother. They had no way of knowing that Joseph would make the demand he did.

Judah then made a promise to be responsible for Benjamin, so Jacob finally conceded and agreed for him to go along. But Jacob insisted that gifts be taken to the Egyptian official, along with the money they had brought back and adequate money for a new purchase of grain. Thus they went again to Egypt.

Second meeting with Joseph (43:16–34).—When they arrived, Joseph arranged for his brothers to dine with him. That turn of events was so unexpected that they thought they were about to be accused of stealing and reduced to slavery. They tried to explain about the money to the steward whom Joseph had put in charge of preparing for their dinner. They described what had happend and insisted that they had brought back the money. They offered to give the money to the steward as evidence that they had intended no dishonesty.

The steward assured them that the money was no cause for concern. They had nothing to fear, for he had received the money himself when they paid for the grain on their earlier trip (43:23). His explanation of what had happened was "God . . . must have put treasure in your sacks for you." Their bewilderment must have been increased even more when, in addition to their kindly treatment, Simeon was released to join them. It seems clear that Joseph had instructed the servant carefully about what he was to say and do.

When noon arrived and they met with Joseph, he inquired about their father. They reported that Jacob was well. The presence of Benja min was almost more than Joseph could bear and still keep his identity concealed. He was so moved that he went aside from them and wept, but he regained his composure and maintained it until he could work out the completion of the testing he had planned.

Egyptian custom was carefully followed in their dining arrange-ments. The Egyptians sat apart when eating to guard their ritual purity. Joseph ate alone in keeping with his high official position. The brothers ate together, and they were amazed that the seating had placed them by ages from the eldest to the youngest. They noticed and must have wondered how anyone in Egypt could have known their complex birth order, since they were born to four different mothers. They still had no hint of who Joseph was, so they would never have dreamed that he was the source of that information.

The climax of the testing (44:1-34).—Joseph kept in control of the situation, knowing what he planned to do in the end. He ordered that preparations be made for their return home. They were supplied with grain. Their money was put back into their bags just as it had been before. In addition, Joseph's personal silver cup was placed in Benjamin's bag. Then they were sent on their way.

The significance of the cup should not be overlooked. It was de-scribed as the cup from which "my lord drinks, and by this that he divines" (44:5). The use of a "divining cup" was a quite common practice in ancient Oriental cultures. The cup was filled with water or oil; an object was dropped into it; and the diviner would interpret the future by the movement in the liquid created by the falling object.[6] As such, a sacred character was attributed to a divining cup; and to steal one was a very serious crime.[7] The penalty was usually death or enslavement.

Was Joseph playing a cruel game with his brothers as has been suggested?[8] No; he was seeking to learn how they would respond when confronted by decisions that involved their own interests and those of others.

When they were only a short way on their journey, Joseph sent men to overtake them, find the silver cup, and bring them all back to appear before him again. That was a part of Joseph's planned test of the brothers. He had set the stage for the final act of that testing.

He would see if they really did care about their father or about Benjamin who was Rachel's son and only their half-brother.

When they were confronted by Joseph's steward, they protested their innocence and expressed complete bewilderment at the incredible things that had happened. They vowed that if any one of them had taken the cup, that one should die and the rest would become Joseph's slaves. Apparently with Joseph's instructions, the steward responded that only the guilty one would be enslaved. Then a search was made, and the cup was found in Benjamin's sack.

They were brought back to appear before Joseph. There Judah acknowledged their obvious guilt. The cup had been found among them, and they could not deny it. It would be nothing more than apparent justice if all of them were made slaves. Again Joseph declared that only the guilty one would be punished, while the rest would be free to go home to their father. The culminating blow had been struck. Would they abandon Benjamin and go home to report his loss, as years before they had reported Joseph lost?

Consider the utter frustration they must have felt—knowing they were innocent of all the unexplainable things that had happened, but being unable to prove their innocence or convince this mysterious official whom they could not understand. Was Joseph punishing them by the drawn-out suspense? No; he had an important purpose in what he was doing. The brothers, on the other hand, were convinced that God was continuing to punish them for their evil of years before (44:16).

While no reference to it is made in the text, the reader is reminded of the parallel distress Joseph had experienced some years before when he was in the Egyptian prison. He too was innocent of the charges against him. He had not done what Potiphar's wife had accused him of doing, but he could not prove his innocence or gain release from the prison. God had helped him through, however, and now he would be God's servant to show mercy to his brothers.

Judah proved the genuineness of his compassion and integrity. He reported to Joseph the conversation the brothers and Jacob had had about Benjamin. He described how Benjamin was the son on whom Jacob's heart and hope rested; "his life is bound up in the lad's life" (44:30). Judah knew that Jacob's heart would be broken if they returned without Benjamin—so much so that he would probably die in his sorrow. And Judah cared.

He then volunteered to take Benjamin's place. He asked Joseph to let him become the slave so Benjamin could return home with his brothers. Judah had been the one who finally persuaded Jacob to let Benjamin come with them to Egypt. He had made the promise, probably rash but inescapable, that he would bear the blame for the rest of his life if he did not see Benjamin safely home again. Judah knew that he could never get away from the consequences of going home and leaving his brother in Egypt. There is intense pathos in his words "For how can I go back to my father if the lad is not with me?" (44:34).

Judah was the brother who had suggested that Joseph be sold into slavery so the brothers could be rid of him and gain a profit for themselves at the same time (37:26–27). Now he was ready to become a slave himself to live up to his promise and protect his father from further sorrow. Centuries later a descendant of Judah, Jesus of Nazareth, took the guilt of others upon himself so he could redeem them and restore them to their heavenly Father.

Joseph identified himself (45:1–20).—It was enough. Joseph could stand it no longer. He sent all his Egyptian servants away so he could be alone with his brothers. Then he told them who he was. They were dumbfounded, and understandably so. They simply could not believe their ears. No doubt they were struck with a new sense of anxiety, wondering how Joseph was going to deal with them for what they had done to him. Again, however, the guilt and dismay were their own. Joseph was not using the past to punish them and gain personal vengeance. He called them to himself and told them again the incredible truth. He was Joseph their brother. He was trying to get that truth to sink in so they could accept it.

Joseph revealed insight and forgiving compassion. He did not pretend that what they had done was good or right. He confronted the issue in its reality. They had sold him into slavery, but God had overruled their evil intention and made good come out of it. Joseph insisted that they not punish themselves with guilt any longer. Instead, they should rejoice because God had used that tragic event of the past to make a providential thing happen for all of them.

There was no question in Joseph's mind that God had been active in the events of his life. It is equally certain that God had not prevented people from doing evil things. Joseph's brothers and Potiphar's wife had done genuinely bad things to Joseph. God had sustained him, however, and in spite of the evil done he had made a channel through which providential good had taken place.

An emotion-filled reunion took place, but Joseph would not linger over it. His thoughts turned to their aging father and their hungry families. Word must be taken to them, along with needed provisions. Joseph spoke immediately, as if he had already planned it, of arranging for Jacob and all the clan to move to Egypt where he could provide for them.

Word spread through the land of Egypt that Joseph's brothers were there. Pharaoh was pleased when he heard that news, and he agreed with Joseph's plan to relocate Jacob's clan in Egypt.

The migration (45:21 to 47:12).—The king furnished wagons and supplies for the migration journey. Jacob's sons took them and went to bring their father and their families to Egypt. Jacob was simply overwhelmed by the news when he heard it. He could not believe that Joseph was really alive. Only the wagons that the Egyptian pharaoh had sent to bring him to Joseph in that far-off land were concrete enough evidence to finally persuade Jacob that he was not just dreaming. So he said with resolve, "I will go and see him before I die" (45:28).

Jacob was ready to go and see Joseph and live with him, but he had reservations about leaving the land of Canaan again to go to Egypt. He remembered how his grandfather Abraham had insisted that his father Isaac not be taken out of the land (24:6). He also remembered how God had told Isaac not to leave Canaan and go to Egypt (26:2). And he remembered how his journey to Haran, planned for a short time, had turned into years (27:43-45; 31:41). His hesitation to make this migration out of Canaan was justified, for Jacob returned to Canaan only when he was brought back after his death for burial at Hebron. His family and descendants left Egypt and returned to Canaan only after the Exodus more than four centuries later.

So when Jacob came to Beer-sheba he stopped. He needed assurance that God's covenant would be continued to him if he left the land and went to Egypt. Jacob left Beer-sheba and went on toward Egypt only after a message had come from God giving him permission to go and assuring him that God would go with him (46:1-4). Jacob then moved on with his clan and possessions, assured of God's blessing and anticipating a reunion with Joseph. The total number of the clan, including Joseph's sons who had been born in Egypt, was now seventy persons (46:27).

Upon their arrival, Jacob sent Judah to Joseph to let him know they had come to the land of Goshen. Joseph came quickly to meet his father, and they had a joyful reunion. Jacob declared that he was ready to die. His life was full; he had seen Joseph again.

Joseph then began to lay out his plans for settling the family in the land. First, they would go to the pharaoh and let him know they had arrived. Very likely that trip would take them to the northern delta city of Avaris,[9] for historical evidence indicates the Egyptian capital was there at the time of this migration.

In the period just before 1700 B.C., a major invasion of Egypt occurred. A wave of Canaanite and Semitic people called Hyksos overran Egypt and established a new dynasty and a powerful empire.[10] The migration of the Israelite clan probably occurred during a time of continued movement of people from Canaan to Egypt due to the famine. Such an unsettled military situation may have explained why the Egyptians were so suspicious of anybody who might be a spy (42:9).

Joseph's plan was to gain permission from the king for the Israelites to settle in the land of Goshen. That would be an ideal place for them to live. The land there was fertile and would provide good grazing. They would be near enough to the capital that Joseph could watch over them and provide for them (45:11).

From the point of view of the king, however, it would be unwise to settle foreigners along the border region of the land. In case of military invasion, foreigners might choose to help the invaders. Since the rulers at that time were Semitic Hyksos, they were probably less afraid of the Israelites than a native Egyptian ruler would have been.

In order to get his family settled where he wanted them, Joseph coached his brothers in what they were to say (46:31–34). He would present his father and brothers to the king. He was sure the pharaoh would ask about their occupation before deciding where to let them settle. Joseph told them to report that they were shepherds. The king would consequently want to settle them in an area away from the main part of Egypt. That would lessen the likelihood of conflict with the Egyptians, who thought that shepherds were a lower class of people than settled farmers. From Joseph's point of view, it would also reduce the likelihood of intermarriage and Egyptian influence on the Israelites.

The result turned out as Joseph had planned. Jacob and his sons were presented to the pharaoh. They reported that they had brought their herds to Egypt with them and wished to sojourn in the land. The king welcomed them and gave Joseph instruction to settle them in Goshen. He even asked that some of the best herdsmen of the family be put in charge of his own herds of cattle. He was apparently convinced that these experienced herdsmen would manage his cattle well and gain a healthy increase.

The Israelites went to Goshen and settled with their families. The migration was complete. Egypt would be home to the Israelites for a long time before their Exodus and return to Canaan would come.

The Last Years of the Famine (47:13–26)

The severity of the famine increased. First of all, Joseph sold grain to the people from the stored reserves for money. When all their money was exhausted, he then furnished them grain in exchange for the ownership of cattle and other livestock. The reference to horses (47:17) is interesting, for it is the first mention of horses in the Bible.[11] This supports the date for these events at about 1700 B.C., since it was at the time of the Hyksos invasion that horses and chariots were first brought into Egyptian life.[12] There is no indication that all the livestock was gathered into huge royal herds. Apparently ownership was transferred to the king, while the people continued to herd them as tenants.

As the famine continued, the people had to resort to selling their lands and themselves to secure grain for food. They readily agreed to indenture themselves to the king to avoid starvation in the famine. Before the famine ended the pharaoh owned all the land in the nation except the lands of the priests. They had an established allowance from the king and so were not forced to sell their lands to buy food.

When the famine did end, Joseph then gave the people seed grain as well as food so they could plant the land again. It may have seemed cruel for the people to be reduced to slavery by the misfortune of a famine. The terms of their service were not severe, however. The king owned both lands and people, but in reality Joseph only made tenants of them. They were to pay 20 percent of their harvests as rentals. By contrast, private business transactions often had much higher interest rates.[13] The people did not feel that they had been mistreated. Rather, they expressed gratitude to Joseph for having been saved from starvation.

Jacob's Last Years (47:27 to 50:14)

Jacob was 130 years old when he migrated to Egypt. He was easily established in favor with the Egyptian king because he was Joseph's father. Jacob and all his clan were provided for through the famine years by Joseph out of the grain reserves he controlled.

After the famine years, prosperity came again to the land and to Jacob. He lived for seventeen years after he migrated to Egypt and settled there. When he sensed that the end of his life was approaching, Jacob asked Joseph to promise that his father would be taken back to Canaan for burial in the cave at Machpelah with his fathers.

Jacob's blessings (48:1 to 49:27).—Joseph brought his sons Manasseh and Ephraim for their grandfather to bless them before his death. The depth of emotion felt by the aged Jacob was expressed in his words "I had not thought to see your face; and lo, God has let me see your children also" (48:11). Jacob's life was indeed full of richness in his last days. Joseph intended for Jacob to place his right hand on the head of Manesseh and give him the primary blessing because he was the older of the two sons. But Jacob crossed his hands and put his right hand on the head of Ephraim. Joseph objected, but Jacob insisted that Ephraim would be the stronger. Jacob had never been very impressed with the importance of the order of birth. With his grandsons, as with himself, he was more concerned about strength of character and leadership.

Jacob also gathered all his other sons and spoke blessings on them before his death. In each blessing the aged father described the character of the sons. He made a prediction of how each one of them would turn out, and these were prophetic. They were based on insight into the life and future of each of the sons. We can surely believe that the insight of the patriarch was inspired. Reuben was set aside with finality from his preeminent place as the firstborn of the family (49:3–4). Joseph, the firstborn of Rachel, was given the status of priority.

The blessing of God Almighty would be added to the blessing of his father to make him rich and fruitful (49:22–26). When this last patriarchal act of blessing his sons was completed, Jacob died.

Jacob's burial (50:1–14).—Joseph set about to do what he had promised his father he would do. Jacob was embalmed, and a lengthy period of mourning followed. The Egyptians joined in the mourning because of the prominence Jacob had as the father of Joseph.

The king consented for Joseph to take the adults of the clan and go to Hebron on a funeral pilgrimage. He sent along a military escort. The children and the clan's possessions were left behind. After the mourning and burial they all returned to Egypt.

Joseph's Last Years (47:13 to 50:26)

Joseph's prominence continued through the famine years and on until his death. When Jacob was blessing his sons before his death, he gave the choice blessing to Joseph. Blessing and prosperity would be his future, as lasting as the eternal mountains and as full as the bounties of the everlasting hills (49:22–26).

With that blessing Joseph's father left him, and with that blessing he lived out the remainder of his days. His influence in the land evidently continued even after prosperity returned.

Joseph's fearful brothers (50:15–21).—After Jacob's death, the brothers feared that Joseph would turn on them and take vengeance for what they had done to him in his youth. So they sent a message to him and told him that what they asked was a request of their dead father Jacob. The request was that Joseph forgive their jealousy and cruelty of those years before.

Joseph was moved to tears that they were still carrying such a burden of guilt about something that had happened so long ago. He urged them not to fear. He told them again how God had overruled their intended evil and made it turn out good. To hold grudges was not appropriate for people who had received such rich blessings from God. At last the reconciliation was complete. He had forgiven them. He urged them to forgive themselves.

Joseph's death (50:22–26).—Joseph died at age 110. He was something more than 17 when he was sold as a slave and taken to Egypt (37:2). He was 30 when he entered the service of the king of Egypt.

For 80 years he served God, his people, and the Egyptians; and he saved many people from suffering and death by starvation. He helped change the course of the history of nations by the movement of the Hebrew clan to Egypt

And then Joseph died. Before his death ne did not ask to be taken to Canaan for burial at that time. The Egyptians would not have favored that. But he foresaw that someday God would lead his people back to the land of Canaan. So he told his brothers to carry his remains with them when that return migration did take place and then to bury him in the land of his fathers.

Joseph was embalmed when he died. In the Exodus the people carried his body with them and buried him at Shechem, in the plot of ground that Jacob had bought there when he first returned from Haran after his years in Laban's household (Josh. 24:32; Gen. 33:19).

Joseph was not an Israelite patriarch in the same sense that Abraham, Isaac, and Jacob were. Abraham was the originator of the covenant nation of God's people. Ishmael and Esau were set aside, so the covenant line was continued through Isaac and Jacob. With the coming of Jacob's sons, however, the covenant was continued to all of them. They were not all set apart except one and the covenant heritage traced through that one.

God had promised Abraham that he would make his covenant a continuing covenant, even an everlasting covenant (17:7–9). Through the nation of Israel, including all twelve tribes of the descendants of Jacob, God worked down through history to fulfill that promise.

The death of Joseph concluded the record written in the book of Genesis. But it did not end the story of God's activity in history with his people. Only a chapter was ended. The marvelous story was continued in the Exodus and throughout the entire biblical account of the gospel of the grace of God.

Notes

1. Gerhard von Rad, *Genesis* (Philadelphia: The Westminster Press, 1972), p. 296.
2. Charles M. Laymon, ed., *The Interpreter's One-Volume Commentary on the Bible* (New York: Abingdon Press, 1971), p. 26.
3. Von Rad, pp. 366–377.

4. Laymon, p. 28.

5. Von Rad, p. 382. See also Henry J. Flanders, Robert W. Crapps, and David A. Smith, *People of the Covenant* (New York: The Ronald Press Co., 1963), p. 106.

6. Laymon, p. 29.

7. D. Guthrie and J. A. Motyer, eds., *The New Bible Commentary, Revised* (Grand Rapids: William B. Eerdmans Publishing Co., 1970), p. 110.

8. Von Rad, p. 391.

9. G. Ernest Wright and Floyd V. Filson, *The Westminster Historical Atlas to the Bible* (Philadelphia: The Westminster Press, 1945), pp. 28, 31.

10. Ibid., pp. 27–28. See also Flanders, Crapps, and Smith, pp. 106–107.

11. James Strong, *The Exhaustive Concordance of the Bible* (New York: Abingdon-Cokesbury Press, 1951), p. 492.

12. Wright and Filson, p. 28. See also James Hastings, *Dictionary of the Bible* (New York: Charles Scribner's Sons, 1954), p. 363.

13. Von Rad, p. 411.

Conclusion

So the book of Genesis ended. But the end was only the end of a phase in God's dealing with his people. The story would go on. God had made a beginning. He created and developed a world. He populated it with creatures of all sorts, including mankind, the moral creatures.

The story of human beginnings is a story of nobility and tragedy, of godliness and sinfulness. It is a story of people and their relationships with God. It is a story of pilgrimage from the Garden of Eden to Canaan to Egypt.

The human family spread and developed into clans and nations. Harsh animosities arose among them because of conflicts like those between Cain and Abel, between Jacob and Esau, and between Joseph and his brothers. The search for brotherhood and peace is as old as human history.

And God's search for a faithful people has gone on just as long. He who called Adam in Eden, called Abraham from Chaldea, met

Jacob at Peniel, and guided Joseph in Egypt was the eternal God. They called him El Shaddai, God Almighty (17:1). He was Creator and King. He is always sovereign. He is graciously kind.

The ongoing record of God's active work among his people would continue with the story of the Exodus from Egypt and national life in the promised land of Canaan. There would be both faithfulness and unfaithfulness on the part of the covenant people. But God would prove to be unfailingly good and faithful. The story of God and his people would finally include the greatest of all good news, the gospel of Jesus Christ, Son of God.

From God's beginning work, there have come the world he is still moving toward its final end and the people whom he is calling upward in a covenant of righteousness. But God was only beginning. He had made the world's genesis and ours. Because of those beginnings, all that has followed has been filled with the qualities of excellence and grace. God always makes it so, and "he who began a good work . . . will bring it to completion" (Phil. 1:6).

Bibliography

General Works

Anderson, Bernard W. *Understanding the Old Testament*. Englewood Cliffs:
    Prentice-Hall, 1957.
Flanders, Henry J.; Crapps, Robert W.; and Smith, David A. *People of the
    Covenant: An Introduction to the Old Testament*. New York: The Ronald
    Press, 1963.
Heaton, E. W. *Everyday Life in Old Testament Times*. New York: Charles
    Scribner's Sons, 1956.
Manson, T. W. *A Companion to the Bible*. New York: Charles Scribner's Sons,
    1947.
Wright, G. Ernest, and Filson, Floyd V., eds. *The Westminster Historical Atlas
    to the Bible*. Philadelphia: The Westminster Press, 1945.

Commentaries

Francisco, Clyde T. "Genesis," *The Broadman Bible Commentary* 1 rev. Nash-
    ville: Broadman Press, 1973.
Fritsch, Charles T. *Genesis: The Layman's Bible Commentary* 2. Richmond:
    John Knox Press, 1959.
Kidner, Derek. *Genesis: Tyndale Old Testament Commentaries*. London: The
    Tyndale Press, 1967.
Simpson, Cuthbert A. "Genesis," *The Interpreter's Bible* 1. New York: Abingdon
    Press, 1952.
Von Rad, Gerhard. *Genesis: The Old Testament Library*. Philadelphia: The
    Westminster Press, 1976.